Bully

An Adventure with Teddy Roosevelt

By JEROME ALDEN

A LOU REDA BOOK
CROWN PUBLISHERS, INC., NEW YORK

This play starred JAMES WHITMORE as Theodore Roosevelt.

It was first performed on February 10, 1977, at the Playhouse Theatre, Wilmington, Delaware, produced by George Spota/Four Star International. It opened at the Forty-Sixth Street Theatre, New York City, on November 1, 1977, produced by Cathy Rait, Kevin Krown, Don Saxon. It was directed by Peter H. Hunt. Setting and costumes by John Conklin. Lighting by Peter H. Hunt.

All photographs from the original production by Ken Howard.

©1979 by Jerome Alden

All rights reserved. No part of this book may be reproduced or utilized in any form or by any means, electronic or mechanical, including photocopying, recording, or by any information storage and retrieval system, without permission in writing from the publisher.

Inquiries should be addressed to Crown Publishers, Inc.,
One Park Avenue,
New York, N.Y. 10016

Printed in the United States of America

Published simultaneously in Canada by
General Publishing Company Limited

Library of Congress Cataloging in Publication Data

Alden, Jerome.
"Bully" : an adventure with Teddy Roosevelt.

1. Roosevelt, Theodore, Pres. U.S., 1858-1919—Drama.
I. Title.
PZ4.A356Bu [PS3551.L33] 812'.5'4 79-1390
ISBN 0-517-53786-9
ISBN 0-517-53787-7 pbk.

Designed by Ruth Kolbert Smerechniak

This play is dedicated to the reality that was Jeffrey Alden . . . by his father . . . Barbara, his mother . . . his sister, Jennifer . . . his brothers Christopher and David . . . plus all the others who loved him, respected him . . . and have not forgotten.

"He was a gleam of teeth and a flash of glasses!"

"He wore for the most part the black slouch hat he bought when he was Police Commissioner of New York City. And except for extremely formal occasions—such as reviewing the fleet or some state function (while in the White House)—he wore his slouch hat and his business suit. No white-vested, black-string-tied, gray-trousered McKinley in his Prince Albert coat."

"And though he pronounced 'A' with a broad accent and 'R' with a soft roll, he spoke with a kind of suppressed vehemence. When excited his voice would shift involuntarily from a resonant tenor to a shrill falsetto . . . later he learned to use this when he came to the punch line of a joke . . . the voice rising to the humor and pushing out the joke in a cracked crescendo of shrill falsetto!"

"The vehemence of his public speaking—which was caused in part by a physical difficulty of utterance . . . the sequel of his early asthmatic trouble . . . and in part by his extraordinary vigor, created among some of his hearers who didn't know him, the impression that he must be a hard drinker or that he drank to stimulate his eloquence!"

"TR's attitude as a speaker, his gestures, the way in which his pent-up thoughts seemed almost to strangle him before he could utter them, his smile showing the white row of teeth, his fist clenched as if to strike an invisible adversary, the sudden dropping of his voice and leveling of his forefinger as he became almost conversational in tone, and seemed to address special individuals in the crowd before him, the strokes of sarcasm, stern and cutting, and the swift flashes of humor which set the great multitude in a roar . . . became familiar to millions of his countrymen; and the cartoonists made his features and gestures familiar to many other millions."

(from his contemporaries)

INTRODUCTION

by THEODORE ROOSEVELT IV

Writing a play about a recent historic figure is a difficult task. Since the outlines of the figure have not been obscured by the mists of time, the playwright is denied the use of poetic license in creating his work. When the figure is as multifaceted as Theodore Roosevelt, and has been the subject of intense analysis by historians, the task virtually becomes a dramatist's nightmare. "Bully" succeeds. It is a first-rate play that meets the historian's standards of accuracy.

Yet, it is precisely because Theodore Roosevelt was a modern president that many of the principles he sought to establish are pertinent today. Issues such as conservation, judicious diplomacy, and the role of the federal government in regulating business are, if anything, more relevant now than they were during his lifetime. "Bully" does not resolve these issues for us, but it admirably captures the spirit of the first American president to wrestle with them.

Act One
The Adventures of Theodore Roosevelt

Act Two
The Further Adventures of Theodore Roosevelt

His Viewless Companions

Elihu Root	Secretary of War
Henry Cabot Lodge	Senator from Massachusetts
Jules Jusserand	French Ambassador
H. L. Mencken	Critic, *Baltimore Sun*
Edith Carow Roosevelt	Second Wife
William Allen White	Publisher, *Emporia Gazette*
Gifford Pinchot	Governor of Pennsylvania, Conservationist
Theodore Roosevelt, Sr.	Father
Martha Bulloch Roosevelt	Mother
Joe Murray	New York City Politician
Alice Hathaway Lee Roosevelt	First Wife
"Bink"	Quentin's Friend
Quentin Roosevelt	Son
Bill Loeb	Private Secretary
Baron Jutaro Komura	Emissary of the Mikado
Minister Kogoro Takahira	Emissary of the Mikado
Mrs. Curtis	Visitor to the White House
Count Serge Witte	Emissary of the Czar
Kermit Roosevelt	Son
Alice Roosevelt	Daughter
Theodore Roosevelt III	Son
Ethel Roosevelt	Daughter
Archie Roosevelt	Son
President Woodrow Wilson	

ACT ONE

The curtain is up, and the audience is able to absorb the essence of the North Room at Sagamore Hill. In it are the various physical fragments of THEODORE ROOSEVELT*'s life:*

A desk with papers and books and a vintage 1900 telephone.

A table filled with memorabilia and more books, surrounded by two chairs with leopard skins thrown over their backs.

Upstage two giant elephant tusks stand in front of a balustrade, and behind that, pillars frame an entrance that seems to stretch out to infinity.

Downstage left is part of a rowboat with oars.

Downstage right are three logs of different sizes and shapes on which he can hack away with an ax from time to time—or on which he can simply sit. On one log is a Teddy bear.

Hanging above all these fragments—in limbo—are stuffed heads: moose, deer, grizzly bear, etc. They stare down at us from a dusty past.

When the audience is seated, the lights dim, the opening music begins. After a moment, there is a loud, roaring, good-natured laugh from the back of the theatre. The stage lights come up bright and glowing, and down the aisle . . . comes TR.

HE *charges briskly down the aisle to the front of the orchestra wearing a khaki riding outfit terminating in brown boots. On his head is the perennial campaign hat. His hands are gloved.*

As TR *moves down the aisle with his group of "unseen friends,"* HE *keeps up a running chatter, alternately cajoling and pointing out various things.*

All right, gentlemen, close it up! Close it up! Have to help each other through this one. No, Congressman, can't go around—got to go through! Here, give me your hand. That's it! That's it! There we go! Fine. All right boys, follow me! Onward, onward. We're on the last lap. Don't drag, don't lag, gentlemen. . . . What's that, Senator? That bird? Oh, that's *Dolichonyx oryzivorus* . . . Icteridae family. Bobolink to you, Senator:

> "Bob-o-link, bob-o-link
> Spink, spank, spink . . ."

(HE *moves down the aisle toward the stage, suddenly realizes somebody's missing.)*

Where's Root? *(Turns and looks back)* Elihu, what're you doing sitting in that mud puddle? For heaven's sakes, you can't rest now, man. . . . We're almost there.

(HE *rushes up to help the man.)*

Oh you slipped. Well come on, up up up. Up you go. There you are. *(Looking down)* Oh, I must say you picked a royal spot to sit, Root. Oh yes. *(Reaches down and comes up with a small delicate flower)* See this little blue flower? Royal flower. *Gentiana Andrewsii.* Named after the king of Ilyria—Gentius. That's of course where Shakespeare laid his play *Twelfth Night.*

(HE *moves back down the aisle gazing at the tiny blue flower, reciting:)*

Thou blossom bright with autumn dew
And colored with the heaven's own blue.

(HE *practically "bumps into" the stage. Then turns around with a boyish, devilish grin.)*

Here we are, gentlemen. Going to be a bit of a problem here. *(Grins)* Obstacles, always obstacles. *(Sees somebody)* No no Congressman! Can't go around. Got to go up and over, always up and over. That's a good lad. Here. I'll give you a hand. *(As if pushing somebody up onto the stage)* Up . . . you . . . go. *(Turns)* All right, now you, Elihu. There you go . . . you can do it. *(Hauling and pushing)* Fine. Fine. *(To someone else)* Now . . . oh, you can do it yourself Congressman. . . . *(Watches the man climb up onto the stage)* Good for you. Bully. Bully.

All right, everybody—let's go: up and over. Up and over.

(TR *climbs up and onto the stage, hauling other people up right and left behind him. Then* HE *charges over, into, and out of the rowboat, rushes around the desk, and finally comes to an energetic halt center stage, throwing out his arms in a grand gesture of glowing triumph.)*

We made it!

(HE *stands puffing for a moment, satisfied and grinning. Teeth gleaming, eyeglasses flashing ... looking like a steamroller in trousers.)*

Bully! Bully! *Finis coronet opus,* "the end crowns all"; "may the last be the best!" By Godfrey, it was deelightful. Deeeelightful. I'm proud of you all. *(Suddenly looks down)* Senator, what're you doing down there on your hands and knees? *(Bends down to pet the senator like a puppy)* No no no, stay there, stay there. Great Scott, you deserve to stay in that humble position for a little while. We traversed more than five miles today! Stay and catch your breath. *(To someone else)* Yes, yes, Congressman, Sagamore Hill is glorious this time of year. Trees are lovely, but you must go as I told you to Yellowstone Park. Get to California. Why they have trees out there so tall it takes two men to look to the top of them: one looks till he gets tired, then another commences where he left off and carries on to the top!

That's right, and we've got to save them, gentlemen. If one thing comes out of this walk today, we must— *(Looks down)* how you doing down there Senator—good good. Just take it easy. The breath always—

(Listens ... turns to someone else) I know, Congressman. I know. You're not getting any help from the White House. I wish I were there, but I'm not and that simply means it's up to you fellows. Got to do the job. Need action. Need action, and need it now. By Godfrey, it's 1912 and the century's already getting away from us! Good. Glad we see eye to eye on that, gentlemen. *(Suddenly aware of somebody standing tall beside him,* HE *looks up.)* Good for you, Senator—you're up! Bully. Bully. *(*HE *guides them all, walking across the stage.)* Now, you boys go right up to the house. Edie and the girls'll patch you all up.

Root will show you the way. *(Looks around)* Great Scott, where's Root? (HE *turns, and in a kind of half-squat position of an Indian scout,* TR *peers all around the stage, finally finding his man.)* Elihu? What're you doing sitting in the rowboat? For heaven's sake, get out of it, man.

*(*TR *rushes across to the rowboat to help* "ROOT." HE *reaches into the rowboat, then pulls back abruptly.)*

All right! I won't touch. I won't touch! You did what? Dislocated it? Stand up, Elihu. . . . Stand up. *(Looks)* No no no, it isn't dislocated, I can tell from here. Oh, for heaven's sake, the wet pants won't hurt you, Elihu . . . help ease you into your second childhood, that's all. *(Reaches in gently to help the man out of the rowboat)* That's it. That's it. *(Leads* ROOT *across the stage . . . stomping his foot to demonstrate)* Work it out, work it out . . . like that. Come on. Come on. Well, we're not as young as we were when I was in the White House. Four years is a long time. *(Has reached the other side of the stage)* Now, when you get up to the house, Edie'll put you in a warm tub. Be good as new. Run along, Elihu; I'll be up shortly.

(TR waves good-bye and chuckles as "ELIHU" exits.) Well, there they go, the remnants of my "Tennis Cabinet." The walking wounded.

You know, the seven and a half years I was in the White House, I always tried to get a couple of hours exercise everyday. Sometimes tennis. More often horseback riding. Or else a rough, cross-country walk like you observed here just now. It was up Rock Creek—then as wild as a stream in the White Mountains. Or on the Virginia side along the Potomac. My companions on those walks we got to calling the Tennis Cabinet: officials high and low, foreign ambassadors, cabinet ministers, undersecretaries and oversecretaries. 'Course we pushed out the phrase to include my old-time Western friends, prizefighters, writers, hunters, and others who'd taken part with me in more serious outdoor adventures than just walking for pleasure. *(Winks)* What we'd do, you see, is make a beeline for a point four or five miles off. Rule was . . . anything got in the way, we'd just go over it . . . under it . . . or through it. Even the Potomac, if it was foolish enough to get in our way. *(Laughs at the memory)* Oh yes, we'd just strip down and swim across. 'Course under such circumstances we had to arrange our return to Washington after dark so our appearance wouldn't scandalize the natives. I remember . . . *(Laughs and shakes all over at the memory)* . . . the French Ambassador: Jusserand was his name. Since become a very very dear close friend of mine, but then, the first time . . . I'll never forget it. I invited him to join the Tennis Cabinet. Oh my lord. . . . *(Laughs so hard he has to struggle to catch his breath)* Well, I simply said, "Come join us for a walk, Mr. Ambassador. But somehow "walk" got translated into "promenade," because the French Ambassador arrived at the White House punctually. In formal afternoon dress: silk hat, boutonniere, and lavender kid gloves. As if he was going for a stroll in the Tuileries or on the Champs-Elysées. Well, the rest of us were all decked out in tramping clothes: knickerbockers, boots, the works. But you can't embarrass a human being because of his clothes can you—so we just started right off going pell-mell through the town out into the country.

(TR "mimes" a walker, staying in place, briskly paced.)

Set a good pace: across fields, through bushes, over fences . . . on . . . on . . . always straight forward. M. Jusserand kept right up. If he was winded, he didn't show it. Plucky little devil! Had the honor of "la belle France" in his heart I suppose. *(Giggles)* Well, anyway, onward, onward—into the evening sun ploughed the Tennis Cabinet.

(HE walks right down to the edge of the stage, grinning.)

And then it so happened that on the way home the Potomac River got right smack in our way—by a rather well-planned coincidence, I might add. Well, I looked over at Jusserand and could just hear the wheels going round in his head. *(Imitates, in French accent):*

Aha! We have reached ze goal at
last. Now we are certain to admire
ze river un moment . . . and zen return
ze way we have came.

(Laughs) Well, I said: "Strip! Strip boys! Can't get our clothes wet."

(HE begins removing his gloves and then his jacket, as HE moves across the stage, identifying some of the Tennis Cabinet lined up at the edge of the "river.")

We had Luther Kelly along. Better known as Yellowstone Kelly in the days when he was an army scout against the Sioux: a tall pine tree of a man . . . well, he started unbuttoning. And Abernathy, the wolf-hunter: he was a fireplug . . . he began stripping. And Elihu Root, my secretary of war . . . was very shortly standing there in all his bony splendor. And before you knew it, all of us, including the French Ambassador, were soon naked as jaybirds . . . *(Puts his folded jacket on top of his head with the campaign hat above it . . . grinning)* . . . staring at a rather formidable Potomac River . . . looking like a row of antique bottles lined up on a shelf. And just as we were about to plunge in, I said, "M. Ambassador? M. Ambassador? You haven't taken off your gloves?" *(Grins)* Well, M. Jusserand held up his hands, still with lavender kid gloves on them, and he said, *(French accent):*

With your permission, M. President,
I will keep on ze gloves. Otherwise
it would be embarrassing if we
should meet ze ladieees!

(Roars with laughter) So, we jumped in . . . clothes over our heads . . . and swam across. We never did meet "ze ladieees." *(His French accent whimsical and wistful)* "Un-for-tu-nate-leeeeee."

(The lights change, as TR *laughs warmly to himself, hangs up his coat on a rack, moves to the downstage corner of the stage where he spies the Teddy bear sitting on one of the logs.* HE *picks it up.)*

You know, the other day a fellow said this was the first famous toy of the 1900s. Glorious animals, bears. Of course, the king is the grizzly, *Ursus horribilis.* Known to the few remaining old-time trappers of the Rockies and Great Plains as "Old Ephraim" . . . sometimes as "Moccasin Joe" . . . the last an allusion to his queer, half-human footprints which look as if made by some misshapen giant walking in moccasins.

*(*HE *sits on one of the logs to smile thoughtfully.)*

Grizzly is the king of the game beasts of temperate North America because it's the most dangerous to hunters. And like most other wild animals who've known the neighborhood of man, bears are beasts of the darkness, or at least the dusk and the gloaming. Aside from man, the full-grown grizzly has hardly any foe to fear. I think . . . the closest shave I ever had was "hunting the grizzly."

*(*TR *puts the Teddy bear back on its log, and gets up to "act out" hunting-the-grizzly.)*

One day while camped near the Bitterroot Mountains in Montana I found that a bear had been feeding on the carcass of a moose I'd killed for food. Made up my mind to try to get a shot at it that afternoon, so when the shadows began to lengthen, I shouldered my rifle and started out.

*(*HE *moves cautiously around the stage, using the pieces of furniture as tree, bush, etc. Stalking the bear.* HE *pantomimes shooting his gun.)*

Had to go for about a mile and a half over a windfall, dead timber piled around in crazy confusion, until I finally reached the densely wooded valley at the upper end of which lay the moose carcass. I trod softly under the great branches. It was now already dusk, and the air had the cool chill of evening.

As I neared the clump where the carcass lay, I walked with redoubled caution. Watching. Listening.

(His voice is hushed and reverent.)

Under the great pines the evening was still with the silence of primeval desolation, and the melancholy of the wilderness came over me like a spell. *(Whispering)* Every slight noise made my pulses throb as I stared motionless into the gathering gloom.

Then—I heard a twig *snap!* My blood leapt. Suddenly the great bear stepped out of the bushes. . . . Its bulk seemed unreal. It didn't see me, and silent as the night, it moved toward the moose carcass. As it got almost there, I put a bullet between its shoulders.

(HE fires.)

It rolled over, while the woods resounded with its savage roar! It struggled to its feet and staggered off . . . fell again squalling and yelling.

(HE fires.)

But again he plunged forward, this time at a heavy gallop into a thicket where I lost him.

(HE rushes across the stage.)

I raced obliquely down a hill to cut him off. Suddenly—watch out! There he is! Standing broadside to me . . . scarlet strings of froth hanging from his lips . . . eyes burning like embers in the gloom.

(HE fires.)

I hold true. My bullet enters his thorax. He charges, with a harsh roar of fury, right at me, blowing the bloody foam from his mouth!

Straight at me he came, crashing through the laurel bushes so it was hard to aim. I waited—until he was almost upon me—

(HE fires.)

Aimed for his forehead, but my bullet went low, smashing the lower jaw. . . . Through the hanging smoke . . . first thing I saw was his paw, as it made a vicious side blow at me.

(HE jumps.)

But the rush of his charge carried him past. He fell, leaving a pool of bright red blood where his muzzle hit the ground. He made two . . . three lunges toward me. Then his muscles suddenly seemed to give way. His head drooped. He rolled over . . . and was dead.

(HE puffs . . . hoarse and excited, then says with quiet elation:)

Bully. By George, it . . . was . . . bully.

(The lights change, as TR grins and clicks his teeth and reaches once more for the Teddy bear.)

But it isn't always that way. Oh, no no no, sir. In fact, the saga connected with this little fellow is not so much high drama as low farce.

On the day in question, I'd gone to hunt bear. It was shortly after I'd become President, and some reporters were along . . . and our old guide . . . hunter named Griffith or Griffin . . . can't remember which because he was always called either "Hank" or "Griff." Well now, Hank or Griff or Griffin or Griffith was a skillful hunter. But he was worn out with age and rheumatism, so his temper failed even faster than his bodily strength. It was fortunate that he was suffering from rheumatism and had to carry a long staff instead of his rifle. I say fortunate because if he'd carried his rifle it would've been impossible to stop him from trying to kill every animal he saw, including some endangered species.

Well, about the middle of the afternoon, the old hunter stooped over with a sharp exclamation of wonder. There in the dust were those half-human footprints. "Moccasin Joe," he whispered.

We all froze.

Suddenly we heard a noise. Rustling in the bushes. Closer. Closer. Closer.

Then out toddled a little cub bear.

"Shoot, you damned fool!" yelled the old hunter. "Shoot!"

Well, of course, I couldn't. I wouldn't. I didn't. And fortunately the little cub scampered off. I say fortunately, because if it hadn't, I am convinced the old hunter would have tried to club the poor little thing to death with his wooden staff.

Newspaper fellows gave the story a lot of publicity. Which is all right. I like that. Only politician who doesn't need publicity is a dead politician. Anyway, a cartoon came out showing "the great white hunter" refusing to shoot the cub. A man named Michtom who owned a toy shop over in Brooklyn . . . well, he made a brown plush bear with movable limbs, button eyes . . . called it Teddy's bear. Wrote asking permission to use my name. Wrote him back saying I couldn't imagine what value my name'd have in "the bear business," but he was welcome to it. Did well. Very well. Everybody pirated the idea and now, my word, the country's up to its *gluteus maximus* in Teddy bears!

(Laughs) But look at it. Just look at it a second. Sweet. Gentle. Have to work mighty hard to imagine a more innocent toy, and yet just the other day out in Michigan I'm told that a priest denounced the Teddy as an "insidious weapon leading to the destruction of the instincts of motherhood and eventual racial suicide." Well . . . *(Grins) chacun à son goût.*

(HE laughs to himself. Looks at the Teddy bear. Then at the audience. Then at the Teddy bear. Then at the audience.)

Look sharp!

(Suddenly HE slings the Teddy bear out into the audience.

When it's caught, HE roars with laughter and pounds his right fist into his left palm in a typical TR gesture of emphasis!)

BULLY! BULLY! Good catch! Good catch! Very good catch! By George, you'll make the team! I like that! I like that! Oh yes I do. I believe in rough sports, believe in a strong, vigorous body. Believe more in a strong, vigorous mind, and I believe most of all in character, because that's the sum of the forces that make a man or a woman worth knowing, worth revering, worth holding on to. Play hard, my dear friends, while you play, but don't mistake it for work. Never. When a young fellow is twenty, it's a good thing if he's a crack halfback, but if he reaches forty and he's never been anything else, I feel sorry for him. Got to keep a sense of proportion.

I preach not the doctrine of ignoble ease, but the doctrine of the strenuous life.

The twentieth century, my friends, looms big before us with the fate of many nations, and our nation calls not for the life of ease, but for the life of strenuous endeavor.

If we stand idly by, if we seek merely swollen slothful ease and ignoble peace, if we shrink from the hard contests where men must win at the hazard of their lives and at the risk of all they hold dear, then the bolder, stronger peoples will pass us by and will win for themselves the domination of the world.

Far better it is to dare mighty things, to win glorious triumphs, even though checkered by failure, than to take rank with those poor spirits who neither enjoy much nor suffer much, because they live in the gray twilight that knows not victory nor defeat.

In the words of an old football player: "Don't flinch, don't foul—but, hit the line hard!"

(HE nods to the audience, pleased with himself. As the lights change, TR moves to go into the "North Room."

Just before HE gets to the desk, something HE seems to hear makes him turn abruptly and look up—into balcony.)

What? What'd you say? Wha's that? I heard a . . . wait a minute. Up there . . . "Captain Jinks of the Horse Marines!" Did I hear you correctly? Wait a minute, who is that?

Good of you to speak up young man, I like that. By George, I think I recognize . . . it's . . . Mencken. Henry Mencken. Oh excuse me, quite right . . . *(To audience)* H. L. Mencken. Young newspaper man from Baltimore . . . works for the *Evening Sun* and the *Morning Sun* and the *Afternoon* . . . what's that . . . quite right: has a new magazine called the *Smart Set. (To audience with some sense of comic satire)* The "smart set" ladies and gentlemen, isn't that nice? *(To "MENCKEN")* Well, Henry, it's a pleasure having you here. . . . Oh no, it really is, I prize my enemies! Remember what Mr. Dooley says *(Thick Irish accent):*

Life ain't worth livin'
If ya don't keep yer inimies!

(Laughs) Henry Louis Mencken, reporter, critic, muckraker, and so on. Good to have you here. *(Listens)* Oh, 'course, sorry. "Captain Jinks of the Horse Marines." *(To audience)* Now a man by the name of Ernest Crosby, one of those Tolstoian pacifists, published a book called *Captain Jinks, Hero.* It was a so-called satire, and it was aimed at the man who was then in the White House and who just so happened to be me.

The plot, if that's what it can be called, told about Jinks who fought in the "Cubapines" . . . (rather thinly disguised, don't you think?) Well, this Captain Jinks, in trying to convince himself that on command he would shoot his mother . . . worries himself into an asylum where he's last seen playing with lead soldiers.

(Laughs) No no no, Henry. Great Scott, if you think that's funny, you should hear what my "friends" said about me. You know Colonel Henry Waterson, don't you? 'Course you do. Well, he said I was as kind a dear old gentleman as ever . . . cut a throat or scuttled a ship. *(Laughs)* What? Oh, 'course, 'course I know McLanburgh Wilson. Come on, I know the verse by heart. Yes, well, he said, speaking of me:

> Our hero is a man of peace,
>   Preparedness he implores;
> His sword within its scabbard sleeps,
>   But mercy! how it snores!

(Laughs) Wasn't a sword as you know. It was a big stick—and I never used it in a demagogic way. *(Looks up at "MENCKEN")* No no, I didn't Henry—say what you like—wait, no no! My White House door swung open as easily to the rich as to the poor . . . but not one whit easier for either. Never! Never, Henry! Never did, no no . . . never catered to the horny-handed sons of toil anymore'n I catered to those malefactors of great wealth: the capitalists and the monopolists!

No sir. No class, no group is above the law of this land, and if Capital or Labor attempted to get their demands by violence, I always put it down. *(Listens)* Yes yes, decisively—but *not in a demagogic way!*

Certainly I pushed the Canal through—pushed it right through the Isthmus, Henry—and right through the Congress. Because the world had to have it, that's why! *(Listens)* No, no, I did not consult the Cabinet—didn't even tell them—there was no time. *(Listens)* Yes yes, Congress did debate it, Henry. They did indeed. But while the debate went on . . . so did the Canal! *(Meekly)* But I didn't do it in a demagog—

(Listens) You really believe that—think I'm the "great I am?" Really believe those stories about my publisher sending to the factory for extra copies of the letter "I"?

(Laughs) Great Scott . . . suppose I do make use of the personal pronoun "I" with enough frequency to irritate good persons quite as egotistical as I—that is, if admitting and taking blame for your own ideas and feelings is egotism. Yes, I believe in power, Henry—believe in a strong executive. Don't think any harm comes from the concentration of power in one man's hands, provided that after a definite limited amount of time that power is returned to the people from whom it

sprang. And hopefully untarnished. I believe in the people. Given half a chance, they usually do the right thing, hand that power to the right person. It's you fringe fellows that trouble me. Sometimes the muckraker is as bad as the wealthy criminal class: all of you trying to paint me as the proverbial Irishman at Donnybrook Fair: rather fight than eat. Oh yes, I have a little Irish in me—along with the Dutch . . . English . . . German . . . touch of Italian . . . and on Election Day who knows what? *(Grins)* Like Mark Twain: I'm an American mongrel and glad of it.

(Grins) Makes it easier to snap my tail at both sides of the political spectrum at once. You folks on the Great Left and you folks on the Great Right . . . I tell you, Henry, I have an absolute horror of the lunatic fringe in all reform movements. They're half-charlatan, half-fanatic, and they ruin their own cause by overstatement: did you know the WCTU says the Spanish War, our troubles in the Philippines, civic dishonesty, and social disorder are all due to the fact that Sherry wine is from time to time served in the White House?

You're confused, Henry? 'Course you're confused. You fellows never could decide if I was a conservative-radical or a radical-conservative! *(Laughs)* Of course I treated anarchists and bomb-throwing, dynamiting gentry precisely as I treated other criminals. Murder is murder! It isn't rendered one whit better by the allegation that it's committed in behalf of a "cause."

Oh, the anarchist everywhere isn't just the enemy of system and of progress . . . but the deadly foe of liberty. Anarchy is no more an expression of "social discontent" than picking pockets or wife beating.

(To "MENCKEN") But you chaps never could "peg" me, could you? "Liberal-radical-conservative-populist-progressive-monarchial-imperialist!" But no no, most definitely not the last. No *(To audience)*, seen too many of them. . . . Sometimes I feel if I meet another king I should bite him. Oh my, the more I see of the Czar, the Kaiser, and the Mikado, the more I'm content with democracy, even if we do have to include as one of its assets . . . the American newspaper.

(To "MENCKEN") That's a joke, Mencken. Well, heavens, I like newspaper people. Like them a lot. Put the first pressroom into the White House, didn't I? *(To audience)* By Godfrey, it's generally supposed reporters have no sense of honor. I mean, that's what they say, but I'm here to testify it's not true. No, sir. No, ma'am. Not true at all. *(Grins)* If you treat reporters fairly, they'll treat you fairly. And reporters *will* keep a secret, if you impress upon them that it must be kept. And you tell 'em to tell everybody else they tell—to keep the secret. And you choose the secret you don't want 'em to tell. *(Confidentially)* And don't do it in a demagogic way.

(Listens again to "MENCKEN") Well, thank you. *(Surprised)* Thank you. Yes, people always used to say I was an astonishingly good politician and divined what the public was going to think. Truth is, I didn't divine how the people were going to think, I simply made up my mind what they ought to think, and then did my best to get them to think it. Hmmm? Sure, sometimes I failed, and then my critics said my "ambition o'erleaped itself." Sometimes I succeeded, and then they said I was an uncommonly astute creature to have detected what the people were going to think and to pose as their leader in thinking it. *(Laughs . . . clicks his white teeth)* And then said I *didn't* do it in a demagogic way.

(To "MENCKEN," *sharply)* Great Scott—are we back to the Canal again?! *(Charges over to raise his fist at* "MENCKEN") No, there were no "reporter's secrets" about the Panama Canal. Will you understand once and for all: you could no more make an agreement with those bandito Colombian rulers—than you could nail currant jelly to a wall! Take this down, Mencken. Take this down. Get out your notebook like a good little reporter and take this down. *(Pounding his chest)* I . . . took . . . the . . . Canal. I, Theodore Roosevelt, took Pana—

(Something interrupts him. TR *looks back upstage as the lights come on brightly to reveal "Sagamore Hill.")*

Oh, Edie? Yes my dear—teatime? Yes, teatime. *(To* "MENCKEN") You'll have to excuse me, Mencken. Edie says it's teatime.

*(*HE *walks into the lighted area—turns to the audience for a second.)*

Thank God for tea.

*(*HE *rushes up to the table, glad to get out of that "session" with* "MENCKEN" *for the moment, and smiles at* "EDIE" *as* HE *pours himself a cup of tea.)*

Tea tea tea—glad I wasn't born before tea! *(Notices something)* Oh, Edie . . . good, you brought the mail. *(Looks over some letters)* Oh, here's one from Comrade Gritto. You remember him, my dear . . . one of my Rough Riders. No no no, darling, not one of the college chaps . . . one of the cowpunchers. *(*HE *has opened the letter.)* Seems the old boy's back out West again. *(Reads)* "Dear Colonel, I am in trouble." Oh oh. "I shot a lady in the eye." Oh my word. "But I didn't intend to hit the lady." Good for you, Gritto. "I was shooting at my wife!" *(Listens)* No no Edie ... nothing important ... he was just commenting on his extraordinary ... marksmanship.

("EDIE" starts out.) Where're you going my dear? Oh into Oyster Bay ... fine ... fine ... could you wait a minute ... you can post my letter to Kermit ... just have to finish it. ... *(HE gets his writing pad, and sits in his chair next to the table.)* I told him how Quenty-quee's becoming too funny for anything. About the other day when Quentin got his legs fearfully sunburned and they blistered and how when you held clinic on him, Quenty looked at his scarlet legs and said *(Imitates "QUENTIN")*:

> They look like a Turner sunset,
> don't they, Daddy? Well ... I won't
> be caught this way. "Quoth the Raven,
> 'Nevermore!' "

You know, my dear, I wasn't surprised at his quoting Poe, but I would like to know where the twelve-year-old scamp picked up any knowledge of Turner's sunsets!

(Hears something) Yes, I believe that *is* the doorbell, dear. I'll get— Oh, all right.... Fine.... You answer it and I'll finish this up immediately.

(HE nods "EDITH" out of the room and begins to write his letter.)

Don't worry about the lessons, Kermit old boy. Harvard can't be any more difficult than when I was there. I know you're studying hard. Don't get cast down. Sometimes in life, both at school and afterwards, fortune will go against anyone. But if he just keeps pegging away and doesn't lose his courage, things always take a turn for the better in the end.

You know, my boy, I am having the best time of any man my age in the world. I thought I'd enjoyed myself *in* the White House, and I did indeed, but I am enjoying myself more thoroughly *out* of the White House, and what's more, I am going to continue—

("EDITH" enters.)

What's that, Edith? Who? All three? Here? Elihu Root? William Allen White and Gifford Pinchot? Well, for heaven's sake, show them in, Edie. Show them in.

(HE *puts down his letter and jumps up to greet* "THEM.")

Gentlemen, what a pleasant surprise! Deeeelighted! Deeeelighted!

(HE *shakes hands with* "ROOT.")

Elihu, good to see you—enjoyed our walk the other day immensely. How's the foot? Feel better? Knew it would. Yes, the children're fine.

(HE *pounds* "WHITE" *on the shoulder.)*

Bill, Bill—good to see—yes, yes, Kermit's doing well at Harvard, thank you very much.

(HE *grabs both hands of* "PINCHOT" *in warm greeting.)*

What, Gifford? In the South paddock? Yes, that *is* a new horse . . . very observant of you . . . what Edie? Got him about two weeks ago.

(HE *guides all the* "MEN" *into the room, stands looking at them a moment. From one to the other, with a big gleaming grin on his face. Stomping his feet like a curious stallion.)*

Now boys, I get the distinct impression you didn't come all the way to Sagamore Hill to discuss my children and horses . . . and stare at me like that? *(Looks at* "PINCHOT") Good. That's better. I like that Pinchot: straight to the point. *(Strolls across the room thoughtfully)* What do I think of Mr. Taft as President? Oh, dear. Well, I picked him, didn't I? Picked him and put that giant of a man right into the hot seat. *(Looks up)* Some of my critics said I did it because I always had a hankering for five-hundred-pound bears!

But I believed in him, Pinchot. Believed in him firmly. Been a fine judge. Did a bully job for me administering the Philippines. Was an excellent lieutenant for me when I was president, but that's the point—he has no instinct for leadership and takes his color completely from his immediate surroundings. Taken me four years away from him to realize that.

Besides, Mr. Taft has fallen backwards off the good political wall, and his somewhat cracked bulkiness now rests in the hands of the plutocrats and machine politicians. It's a sad thing—but like Humpty-Dumpty . . .

all the good Republican men aren't going to be able to put Taft back together again.

What's that, Bill? No no no. All I want is privacy. Want to close up like a native oyster. I told the people in 1904 I wouldn't run for president again. . . . Two terms was enough for any one man. . . . I'm certainly not going to go back on my promi—

(Listens) I understand perfectly well what you're driving at, gentlemen, but I will not be a candidate for president again. Well, Pinchot, I don't think it will become necessary to decide whether to accept a nomination of the Republican Convention. . . .

(Strikes a slightly "heroic" pose)

But . . . if the matter of my candidacy should appear in the guise of a public duty . . . then however I might feel about it personally, I would feel I ought not to shirk it. Uhhh . . . why're you smiling, gentlemen? Something funny 'bout that? Well, all right, of course I'll think about it, Elihu. . . . No harm in thinking about anything, is there?

(Rubs his hands together with sudden glee)

Now, boys, suppose before dinner . . . we have a good tramp through the woods—what's that Elihu . . . you can't stay? Got to leave? Foot still a little worse than you thought. Sorry about that.

*(*HE *guides them all up to the balustrade, waving them out . . . lingering to listen to something "*PINCHOT*" whispers to him.)*

What's that Pinchot? Can't hear you?

*(*TR *leans way up. Listens—then roars with laughter.)*

Outrageous! Outrageous! Now go on . . . get out before I wrestle you out!

*(*HE *waves at* PINCHOT, *laughs again to himself, looks at* EDITH *thoughtfully, as the lights change.)*

How 'bout a row, Edie? Think both of us could use a good row on the bay.

(HE *leads the unseen* EDITH *across the stage and over to the rowboat.)*

By George, those blue spruces are doing well over there by the tennis court . . . shooting up . . . spreading out . . . just like the children. *(Points at something)* You know, my dear, your idea of mixing clematis in with the roses should be just lovely come spring. The place should be asplash with color.

("THEY" *have reached the spotlighted rowboat.* HE *helps her in, singing a tuneless kind of song:)*

When you were a tadpole
and I was a fish
in the paleozoic time!

(THEY *are in the boat and seated.* HE *smiles warmly at her and begins to row.)*

You know, Edith, in olden times, rowing used to be the penalty to which galley slaves were condemned. But now it's recommended by athletes as the best of all forms of exercise for developing the body. There's a history lesson in there someplace.

(HE *rows, and begins to laugh uproariously.)*

Oh no, I'm feeling fine, dear. Just laughing at something Pinchot whispered to me before he left. He said, "After TR came Taft. It was as though a sharp sword had been succeeded by a wet roll of toilet paper—legal size!"

Oh, come on, Edie, it's true: Taft's a flubdub with a streak of the second rate in him. Hasn't the slightest idea what's necessary if this country is to make social and industrial progress. Real trouble is his values, like McKinley, Mark Hanna, like most of America's business leaders. They're essentially materialistic. Don't equate America's national interests with the ultimate welfare of humanity. Have the narrow view.

(Rows)

Oh, I've no glory to get out of being president again. Even tho' I march off to church every Sunday behind you, I've no particular assurance there *is* a hereafter. The one thing I want to leave our children is an honorable name. They have that now.

(Stops rowing; they float)

But if I were nominated . . . if I were elected . . . such impossibilities would be expected of me. . . . Don't see how I could avoid causing bitter disappointment to sincere, good people.

But Taft is a flubdub, and I would dearly enjoy sinking my spurs into his rather voluminous flanks and riding him off the range.

Nur der verdient sich Freiheit
  wie das Leben
Der taglich sich eroben muss.

Goethe was right, my dear: "he only earns his freedom and existence, who daily conquers them anew."

(Puts up the oars)

Here, darling . . . let me help you . . . that's it. . . .

(Gets out of the boat)

Hmmmm? No no my dear . . . you go on up to the house. Think'll do a little tree chopping. I want to see which way my *Zeitgeist* is pointing.

(HE starts across to where an ax is implanted in the logs as the lights change.)

No, no, don't worry, Edie—I promise I won't cut down all the trees in the forest!

(TR laughs warmly, and nods her offstage—as he lifts the ax out of the log and begins to chop. The lights have made the mood more reflective.)

(Chops two or three times, then remembers)

You know, my father, Theodore Roosevelt, got a greater joy out of living than any man I've ever known. Performed every duty more wholeheartedly than any man I've ever known. That's a remarkable combination: enjoyment of life and performance of duty.

(HE chops the ax so it sticks into the log.)

He took the children's education very seriously. When I was eleven years old, the entire family went to Europe for the first time. Shortly after that, we children were sent to live with a German family in Dresden for four months, where we learned the language and the culture.

(HE sits on one of the logs.)

It was a family called Minckwitz, and it was there I discovered for the first time, the Norse saga, the *Nibelungenlied.* The book was in Dr. Minckwitz's library . . . and . . . being a frail and sickly child, I was greatly impressed with the exploits of the heroes of the *Nibelungenlied.* Siegfried. Oh, Siegfried.

(HE recites a few words in German, then aware we might not be able to understand, HE recites in English.)

When Siegfried slew the dragon at the
Foot of the mountain, the gallant Knight
Bathed in its blood.
It coated his body so no weapon has pierced
Him in battle ever since.

But a broad leaf fell from the linden
And it stayed gently between his shoulder-blades
It is there, Siegfried can be wounded.

I will take some fine silk, said Kriemhild
And sew a cross on his back that none will notice
And you, Hagen of Troeneck, must shield him
When the battle is fiercest.

But then, as Siegfried bent over the brook
To drink of its cool, sweet water,
Hagen hurled a spear at the cross of silk,
And the hero's blood leapt from the wound.
Siegfried was wounded to death.

(HE begins to struggle to catch his breath. HE removes his glasses and puts

his hand over his eyes. Seems to be having an asthma attack.)

Soon . . . many . . . fair . . . ladies . . . would . . . be weeping . . . for . . . him.

(HE *has a hard time breathing, and finally calls out like a frightened little boy.)*

Papa? Papa?

(Breathes in spurts)

Papa? I can't . . . breathe. Can't seem to . . . get enough . . . air. What, Papa? What? Try . . . to be still? But . . . I can't. I can't. Yes, Papa. I'll try. All right . . . I'll try. . . . Yes, you're right. . . . It is . . . better . . . thank you. Papa . . . will I always have . . . asthma? Will I always be this way? It's . . . up to me? But Papa . . . the doct—yes, Papa, I know . . . God . . . gave me a strong mind, but I must make my own body. I'll try, Papa. . . . I'll try. No . . . I will, Papa. . . . I promise. I . . . will . . . make . . . my . . . body. I will.

(HE *can breathe again now.* TR *gets up from the log and puts his glasses into his pocket, still in the mood of a young boy.)*

I was a nervous, timid youth, unable to hold my own when thrown into contact with other little boys. Yet from reading about people I admired—the soldiers of Valley Forge and Morgan's riflemen to the heroes of my favorite stories—and most importantly, from knowing my father—I felt a great admiration for men who were fearless and could hold their own in the world. I had a ferocious desire to be like them.

(Notices his clenched fists, and HE *moves across the stage, remembering.)*

My first boxing master was John Long, an ex-prizefighter. Oh, I can still see his rooms now: pictures of Tom Hyer and Yankee Sullivan and other great fighters hanging about.

Every year, John Long held what he called "championship matches" for his young charges. I entered, never thinking I could win, because everytime I got the least bit excited my asthma would get the better of me. But this time (HE *grins broadly and breathes very hard once or twice.)* . . . I won. My prize . . . (HE *goes to the desk and gets it.)* . . . was a fifty-cent pewter mug. Been one of my most cherished possessions ever since.

(HE *sees a stuffed bird sitting on the desk. Gets it.)*

When I was thirteen I was allowed to take taxidermy lessons from a Mr. Bell. Tall man, straight as an Indian. Been a companion of Audubon. Excellent teacher. Later, when the family went on a trip up the Nile, I returned with literally hundreds of bird specimens, all of which I stuffed.

(HE *strokes the bird fondly.)*

Mr. Bell didn't only teach me taxidermy, he made me understand the interconnection of all things natural.

(HE *puts the bird back on the desk and comes downstage, glowing with remembrances.)*

It was that same summer that I got my first gun: a breech-loading, pin-free, double-barrel of French manufacture. And something that puzzled me was the fact that my companions seemed to see things to shoot I couldn't see at all.

I had been a clumsy, awkward boy up to that point, and although much of it was undoubtedly due to my general characteristics, a good deal was due to the fact that I couldn't see, and yet was wholly ignorant that I wasn't seeing. It put me under a hopeless disadvantage in studying nature, because the only things I could study were those I ran against . . . or stumbled over.

I told Papa and soon got my first pair of spectacles.

(HE *pulls the glasses out of his pocket and stares at them with whimsy.)*

And now, the world was out there, waiting. Now, the world could be more than just . . . my oyster . . .

(Slams the glasses on his nose)

BAY!

(HE *has made the transformation back from boy to man, and for a moment* HE *grins, clicking his teeth in glee as the lights change.)*

(Looks up) What? Oh, Mencken, that's beneath you. I'm "making a *spectacle* of myself"? Oh, you can do better than that, Henry. So can I? Oh, you mean the pun: "my world . . . Oyster Bay." *(Laughs)* Well, of course it's frightful. Most puns are—that's the point. *(Listens)* No, didn't go to any school, Henry, that's right. All those years I had to be tutored at home. Wasn't healthy enough to go to a regular school. *(Listens)* Yes, I'd say that Harvard was a regular school, but that was later. . . . I'll take that back: Harvard at that time was rather an "irregular" school, if you know what I mean. *(Listens)* You don't. Well, when I entered Harvard in 1876 there was a rather thin patina of sophistication overall, if you know what I mean? Oh you don't. I didn't really fit in because I ran everywhere while my fellow students sort of "strolled." (HE *demonstrates a walk of limp elegance.)* Harvard was a place in transition in a time of rather intense languidity, if you know what I mean. Oh you don't. Well, rather like Bunthorne in Gilbert and Sullivan's *Patience:*

(HE *takes a deep breath, sings, and "prances" about.)*

(Song)

If you're anxious for to shine in the high aesthetic
  line as a man of culture rare,
You must get up all the germs of the transcendental
  terms, and plant them everywhere.
You must lie upon the daisies and discourse in novel
  phrases of your complicated state of mind,
The meaning doesn't matter if it's only idle chatter
  of a transcendental kind.

  And everyone will say
  As you walk your mystic way,
If this young man expresses himself in terms too
  deep for me,
Why what a very singularly deep young man this deep
  young man must be!

(TR *is so tickled with what* HE *is doing*

that HE *begins to exaggerate the "aesthetic" languidity.)*

Be eloquent in praise of the very dull old days which have long since passed away.

(But TR *is caught in the middle of his extreme languidity by the appearance of his* "FATHER.")

Oh! Yes! Father! No no no, sir.

(TR *is embarrassed at being caught fooling around.* HE *quickly adjusts his trousers, pulls them out and over his boots, and rushes over to a clothes rack to get his jacket and put it on.)*

I'll be ready in a minute. I was just having some fun, Father. Just lollygagging around. Oh, yes . . . yes, sir. I have been thinking about it. I've thought of little else. No, I'm not quite sure, sir, but science still interests me the most, I think.

(HE *has on his jacket and buttons it as* HE *comes back downstage to talk to his* "FATHER.")

No no, I'd never . . . I was really just lollygagging, Father. You know I'd never do anything in a dilettantish way. I'd do it seriously, sir—or not at all. Yes, I'm most grateful to you for making it economically possible for me to do pure research if I so choose. *(Listens)* What was that, sir? "Keep the fraction constant." Well, I don't quite underst—well, yes, of course Father, I'll do it. I don't understand what you mean, sir—but I'll do it! *(Listens)* Oh, "If I'm not able to increase the numerator, then I must reduce the denominator." Well, Father, I'm afraid I still don't know what—Oh! Oh, yes sir, now I understand: "if I'm not going to make money, then I have to even things up by not spending any!"

I do understand, and of course, you're right. But Papa . . . Papa . . . please understand . . . I want you to know that whatever I decide to do, I will make you proud of me. I promise.

(Very slight pause)

That was the last serious talk we ever had. My father . . . died . . . in my sophomore year at Harvard when he was forty-six years of age. He was the finest man I ever knew. He was not only a father, but he was the best friend I ever had. After that talk, I was determined to make science my life's work.

(To his "MOTHER" *on the other side of the stage)*

No, Mother. Oh, I know . . . I know . . . but since Papa's death, I've changed my mind. It's Harvard's fault, Mother. It's their attitude toward natural science. They feel that anything not done in the laboratory is unscientific. And I have no more desire to be a microscopist or a section-cutter than to be a mathematician. The nature I want to study is out there—out of doors. The Law? Well, I don't know, Mother. The more I read in books and hear in classrooms, it seems to me that too much of the Law is really *against justice!* Yes, dear, I know there's no rush, but a man does have to get on with it, doesn't he? Well, thank you, Mother, I wish I was as optimistic as you. . . .

(HE *crosses to* "HER," *takes her hand in both of his in a gesture of warmth and affection.)*

But thank you for your confidence. Thank you, darling.

(HE *kisses her "hand." Smiles and watches her exit.)*

Well, I didn't want to be a scientist. Didn't want to be a lawyer. Certainly didn't want to be a businessman.

(HE *moves over to the hat rack to get an early twentieth-century derby hat.)*

So to everyone's amazement, including my own, I decided to enter politics.

(HE *plunks the hat rakishly onto his head.)*

On the sidewalks of New York.

(The lights change, and an offstage piano plays "East Side, West Side." TR *comes forward to tell us how* HE *got into politics.)*

In 1880, a young man of my bringing-up and convictions could only join one party—the Republican Party. But that wasn't as easy as it sounds, because before you could join it—you first had to find it!

When I announced my intentions and began my search some of my friends, the self-appointed haut monde took me aside and said:

East Side, West Side
All around the town
Political clubs are an obscene thing
And socially pull you down.

They're run by horsecar conductors,
Saloonkeepers and sellers of pork.
They'll make you a social pariah
On the sidewalks of New York!

I said: "All right! If that's so, it merely means that you folks don't belong to the governing class, and I intend to be one of the governing class!"

By chance I struck up a friendship with one of the governing class: chap named Joe Murray. Joe had been born in Ireland, come over to America in steerage, and been brought up on the Lower East Side of Manhattan. He became my political mentor. Joe was an eloquent teacher. He said *(Imitates a Lower East Side New York accent)*:

Teodore, you got to get it troo
dose four eyes o yourn dat politics
is a rough game. Tammany runs
everyting in dis town and de district
is Democratic up to its navel, Teodore.
All I do is perform da usual gang woik
for de leader . . . and he gives me my
just reward.

However, after one election, "de leader" showed a callous indifference toward Joe's just reward . . . thinking, of course, that Joe would forgive and forget, but Joe Murray wasn't a man to forgive and forget.

So, as the next election drew near, Joe thought he'd like to make a drive at "de leader" and decided his best bet lay in the race for the New York State Assembly. He picked me as his candidate. *(East Side accent)*

> Teodore, youse shoud've been dere in de
> ballot boots. It was beautiful. You
> know dose guys what come in to vote
> Democratic t'ree, four, five times?
> Well, we trun dem out on dere ears . . .
> and den we picked up dere ballots . . .
> an' slipped 'em to our boys to vote.
> It was beeoooootiful!

(Laughs) Well, the result was, that to the dismay of the Republican machine and "de leader," a twenty-two-year-old boy was sent to the state assembly . . . by the name of Theodore Roosevelt. Now at that time, I wouldn't have thought of running on my own. I didn't have the reputation or ability to win for myself. It wasn't my fight, anyway. It was Joe Murray's *(Grinning)* . . . and I won! *(Sings and dances a waltz clog:)*

> East Side, West Side
> All around the town,
> We jumped over the railroad tracks
> And the walls came tumbling down.
>
> Joe and me together,
> My political stork.
> He gave birth to my whole career
> On the sidewalks of New York.

(HE completes the dance with a rousing finish, laughs, and fans himself with his derby hat as HE walks over to the coat-rack and begins to remove his coat.)

I enjoyed that immensely.

Oh, I know what you're thinking: a rather dubious beginning for a young reformer. And make no mistake about it, I did fancy myself a young reformer. In fact, I burned with the zeal only given to the uninitiated. I was fairly atremble at the prospect of going to the state legislature and setting the world aright. Of course, it was a world, about which . . . for all practical purposes . . . I knew nothing about.

New York Times had only one criticism: "a curable defect called youth." Naturally, my desire was to achieve results and not just issue manifestos-of-virtue. . . . So I eagerly plunged into what some of my friends called "the political swamp," determined to learn how to swim . . . and I did . . . although sometimes I must confess, the stench was almost unbearable.

(HE moves and suddenly sees a gun and holster on a table. Goes to get them.)

To clear my nostrils, I took my first trip West. Discovered the Little Missouri River in the Dakota Badlands and bought some land there. I got my first taste of Western living and I adored it. I . . . don't think I'll ever be able to adequately describe the effects of the great West on the sensibilities of a young Eastern boy like myself.

(Strapping on gun and holster)

It was a land of vast silent spaces, of lonely rivers . . . of plains where wild game stared at a passing horseman. Worked under the scorching summer sun, when the wide plains shimmered and wavered in the heat. Knew the freezing misery of riding night guard round the cattle in the late fall roundup. In the soft springtime the stars were glorious in my eyes each night before I fell asleep. And in winter, blinding blizzards . . . when the driven snow-dust literally burned my face. I felt the beat of hardy life in my veins—the glory of work and the joy of living.

(Suddenly some terrible thought makes him gasp quietly, remembering. The lights slowly change—so the mood is dark and awesome.)

(Quiet-hushed-almost-reverent-anger)

Her name . . . was Alice Hathaway Lee, and I saw her first on October 18, 1878. I loved her as soon as I saw her sweet, fair young face. We were betrothed on January 25, 1880, and married on October 27 of the same year.

We spent three years of happiness such as rarely comes to man or woman.

On February 12, 1884, our baby girl was born. She called it Alice as we planned, kissed it, and seemed . . . perfectly . . . well. Some hours after, not knowing she was in the slightest danger, thinking only that she was falling into a sleep . . . my wife . . . became . . . insensible . . . and d-d-died at t-t-twelve o'clock, February 14, 1884, at 6 West Fifty-seventh Street, New York City.

Beautiful in face and form, lovelier still in spirit; as a flower she grew, and as a fair young flower she died. Her life had been always in sunshine; there had never come to her a single great sorrow; and none ever knew her who didn't love and revere her for her bright, sunny temper and her saintly unselfishness.

Fair, pure, joyous as a maiden. Loving, tender, and happy as a young wife. When she had just become a mother, when her life seemed to be but just begun, and when the years seemed to be so bright before her—then, by a strange and terrible fate . . . death came to her.

And when my heart's dearest died, the light went from my life forever.

And in that same house . . . on that same day . . . my beloved mother died. Why? We . . . buried them both on the same day. Both . . . both. I . . . ran . . . away. Ran . . . West . . . West!

(HE impulsively draws the gun and fires into the air.

Lights come up bright and harsh as HE continues to fire until something stops him.)

(Looking) What . . . Edie? Oh, I'm sorry, my dear. No, no, I'm sorry I startled you. . . . *(Laughs)* No no, I wasn't shooting at Taft. I haven't decided yet to go for the nomination.

(HE puts the gun away sheepishly, back into the holster, as "EDITH" enters. HE follows her over to the armchair where "SHE" is obviously going to sit.)

Quentin's upset? why? Oh, said I promised not to go hunting without him, did I? All right. *(Listens)* No, Edith, I was just thinking through. Remembering . . . and with gratitude. The old West, of course. Owe more to the West and to you than I can ever express. West made me whole again, so I could get over my hurt . . . come back and fall in love with you. By George, we've had a bully life. Bully. I feel I've reached the crest of the wave.

What dear? The men are coming at six o'clock for their answer about my running for the nomination? Great Scott, it's almost that now. Better change . . . get ready.

(HE *quickly removes the gun and holster, moves to the clothes rack to hang them up and get a vest that* HE *puts on thoughtfully, as* HE *comes back to her.)*

Edith? Edith? If it really should be the top of the wave . . . and I begin to go down. All of you who believe in me . . . might be hard for you to see . . . might all leave me . . . but . . . it won't make any difference to you, will it?

You've heard me speak this way before? When, my dear: certainly not when I was police commissioner of New York City . . . enjoyed that immensely . . . why at that time I attempted a novel and revolutionary approach to law enforcement . . . enforcing the law. *(Listens)* When I was vice president. Oh sure. I had ample reason to feel like that as vice president. Remember what Mr. Dooley had to say about the vice presidency, my dear *(Irish accent)*:

It ain't a crime . . . exactly. Ye
can't be sint to jail f'r it.
But the vice prisidency is a kind of
disgrace—like writin'
anonymous letters.

(The remembered frustration sends him back to the clothes rack to get a formal-looking coat to put on over the vest.)

I suppose it's an honorable office, but heavens alive, Edie, I was a young man of forty-two. There was nothing for me to do . . . and I *was* the governor of the state of New York—accomplishing some good things, I felt. But, they did it to me, those malefactors of great wealth—the corporations. I'd beaten them on so many issues they wanted me out of Albany. Oh yes, the machine rolled right over me, and I was nominated and elected, turned out to pasture, Edith, as vice president of the United States of America.

(HE *has on his coat and stands next to the desk.)*

Honestly, I felt as though I were taking the veil.

(Lights abruptly change, so just a pin

spot hits TR*'s face. And there is the sharp distant echo-chambered crack of a gun being fired.* TR *shakes his head, dazed, unbelieving.)*

On September 6, 1901, an anarchist shot and killed President William McKinley in the city of Buffalo, New York.

(The telephone rings. As TR *reaches for the phone, the lights come up bright and gay again.* HE *moves behind the desk and is in the "White House.")*

(On phone) President Roosevelt. Cabot Lodge? Yes put him on. Put him on. Hello, Cabot? Fine thank you, very well. What? No, I hadn't read that. Yes. Read it to me. *(Listens)* Wait wait, hold it, Cabot. Go back. . . . Read me that last part there . . . thing about my posture. . . . Yes . . . that's it . . . "President Roosevelt's craven posture toward Mexico." . . . Mmmm. I see, Cabot, are you sure the Senator said that? You are. Well . . . here's what I want you to do. I want you to go to his office immediately, Cabot. Take a ball bat with you. Hit him smartly between the eyes . . . that's to get his attention. And then inform the man that he's expected here at the White House for luncheon tomorrow at twelve sharp. No no, Cabot . . . he won't be the main course. But Bat Masterson will be here and—

*(A "*LITTLE BOY*" enters.)*

What is it son? *(To phone)* Excuse, me, Cabot, there seems to be a small person here.

*(*TR *puts the receiver on the desk, comes around from behind the desk to bend down to talk to the "*BOY*," who's moved to one side of the stage.)*

Yes, son? Quentin? Well, I'm not sure where Quentin is right now. Oh, he might be over in the gardener's domain, or down by the stables. Quenty got two new raccoons today. Should be building a cage for them. What son, yes, I'll tell him. *(Starts back to desk, turns)* Oh, what's your name? *(Listens)* Spell that for me. B-i-n-k? Bink? Just Bink? That's it? All right, Bink . . . I'll tell him. *(*TR *goes back to the desk, notices a toy* *replica of the Wright brothers' first plane, picks it up.)* Oh, Bink, would you give this to Quentin; he left it here earlier this morn—

(But the "BOY" is gone. TR shrugs and shuffles back to the desk. Picks up the receiver and continues the conversation with "LODGE" as if it hadn't been interrupted.)

(Into phone) Bat Masterson will be here for lunch tomorrow, and he's one of the gentlest men I know. I just want that Senator—that warlike-servant-of-the-people—to realize that strength and bluster are *not* the same thing. No no, Cabot, I'll be very calm and explain to him that our problems with Mexico will not be solved by sending troops. I've put the matter irrevocably before the International Tribunal in The Hague, and that's where it's going to—

(An unseen QUENTIN enters.)

Oh, Quenty-quee. Excuse me, Cabot, Quentin's just come in. *(Puts down the receiver again)* Oh, darling, you've brought the raccoons. Aren't they cunning.

(TR comes out from behind the desk. In a kind of gentle crouch as HE bends over and sticks his hand out to pet the raccoons.)

Yes, let me see them . . . let me . . . *("Raccoon" bites him)* Ouch! *(Sucks his finger)* No no no, that's all right, Quentin. That was just a love nip that's all—little love nip. *(Listens as he continues to suck his finger)* Oh yes, he was. Bink, that's right. That's right: B-i-n-k. He's either over with the gardener or down by the stables. All right, dear. Yes, four o'clock, sharp. Absolutely: pillows at four. Won't fail you, Quenty.

(TR goes back to the desk, sucking his finger. Notices the Wright brothers' model plane, picks it up.)

Oh Quentin, would you—

(But "QUENTIN" *is gone.* HE *sighs, puts down the model plane, sucks his finger, and picks up the phone receiver.)*

(On phone) Cabot? *(Listens)* I'm sucking my finger, Cabot. Yes, just got bitten by one of Quentin's raccoons. Obviously a Democrat!

Now, don't go on about Alice. She's just very spirited. Alice is 19 years old, for heaven's sake! She what? *(Grins with growing glee)* No . . . I hadn't heard that. At the Vanderbilt's party . . . Alice fired a toy pistol with dynamite caps at Mrs. Vanderbilt? No, I don't find it amusing, Cabot—I find it hilarious! *(Roars with laughter)* Oh come on now, Lodge, of course she carries a snake in her purse. I know the snake personally: Emily Spinach is its name. Cunning little thing. *(Listens)* Yes, Emily Spinach. Spinach is for its color. Emily for an aunt of ours who's thin beyond belief.

Now look here, Cabot: I can either be president of the United States, or I can control Alice. I can't possibly do both!

("BILL LOEB" *enters.)*

What, Bill? They are? All right. My goodness. Give me a minute and then show them in. *(To phone)* Cabot, Bill Loeb just told me the Japanese delegation is here, and I have to go. It's rather important. Got to use my good offices to try to stop this terrible war between them and the Russians. Wasteful! Wasteful! Both people and property. But I wish I knew what to say, how to begin.

*(*HE *begins fiddling with the airplane model abstractedly, as he listens.)*

It's not *what* but *how* with the Orientals? Well, my "what" has always been pretty reliable; it's my "how" that gets me in all kinds of trouble. *(Listens)* Oh, that's right, you did meet them! Well, quick, Senator, give me some help. *(Listens)* Inscrutable, are they. That's a big help, Cabot. Well . . . I'll just have to find some way to "unscrute" them, that's all. Oh, here they are! Bye!

*(*HE *hangs up the receiver and bounds up from behind the desk to come around and greet his* "VISITORS."*)*

Come in gentlemen, deeee-lighted. Deeeeelighted. Baron Komura! Mr. Takahira. So nice to see you.

(TR has absentmindedly kept the replica of the Wright brothers' plane in one hand and has been holding it in two hands as HE made ceremonious "bows" in greeting the "JAPANESE." "THEY" see it.)

Oh yes, this . . . it's a toy . . . belongs to my son . . . to Quentin. *(Holds it up so they can see)* A heavier-than-air craft. Some of our boys made it fly for fifty-nine seconds down at Kitty Hawk two years ago. You know, gentlemen, one day, this could become a powerful weapon in warfa— *(Catches himself)* Oh sorry. Sorry. *(Rushes to put it back on his desk)* Now, gentlemen, are your accommodations all right? *(Listens)* Good. Fine. Yes yes, this is where I work. Family lives right upstairs. *(Suddenly thinks of a way to avoid the talk he knows is coming)* By Godfrey, why don't I show you around. Good good. Yes, we're rather fond of the color ourselves. *(He motions them out of the room.)* Oh no, after you, gentlemen. *(Much bowing and bowing)* After you. No no I insist—after you. Oh all right—I'll go first!

(HE bows once more and "pushes" his way between them, guiding them across the front of the stage on a tour of the "White House.")

The place is really too small for us, you know, with the six children, all the dogs, the horses . . . no no we keep the horses outside. We have snakes and two new raccoons *(Waves at someone upstage)* Hello there? You see, we love having people come to see the White House. Excuse me while I say hello to that man over there.

(Goes over and shakes hands with someone)

How do you do, sir? Nice to see you. Enjoy yourself.

(Comes back toward the "JAPANESE." But HE notices that a "WOMAN" downstage is staring at him.)

Excuse me, ma'am. . . . Is something wrong? You seem to be—oh, I see. You're surprised to see me. Well, it's a pleasure. What is your name, ma'am? Curtiss. From Ft. Lauderdale. Oh, forgive me.

(With gentle formality)

Mrs. Curtiss . . . allow me to introduce you to the Japanese Minister of Foreign Affairs, Baron Komura. And this is the Japanese minister to the United States, Mr. Takahira. Gentlemen, this is Mrs. Curtiss of Ft. Lauderdale, Florida. Yes, oh that's bully. Bully bully bully.

What, gentlemen? Oh, well, she just—sorry Mrs. Curtiss. They have a difficult time understanding our accent. *(To* "JAPANESE") What Mrs. Curtiss said was that she's come all the way up from Florida, that's one of our southern states, just to see what a real live president looked like. Well, ma'am, that's very kind of you. We northerners very often go down to Florida just to see a real live alligator!

("BILL LOEB" *enters.)*

What is it, Bill? *(Looks at his pocket watch)* By George it is four o'clock isn't it. *(To* JAPANESE) Gentlemen, you'll have to forgive me—I've a very very important engagement. Now we'll talk tomorrow—go over the whole situation with the Russians. That's right. Eleven o'clock at the State Department. *(To the woman)* Oh, Mrs. Curtiss, would you do me a very big favor—would you mind showing these gentlemen around the White House? You would, good. Thank you, thank you, my dear. *Sayonara,* gentlemen. *Sayonara.*

*(*TR *bows very formally to the* "JAPANESE," *and watches them out of the corner of his eye as* "MRS. CURTISS" *guides them offstage.)*

Dearest Ted, the last few days I've been having terrific pillow fights with Archie, Quentin, and some of their cunning little friends.

*(*HE *reaches down beside the desk and comes up with a pillow from its "hiding place." Then* HE *moves cautiously, with quiet glee, around the stage as if "stalking" some small creature with his pillow.)*

Wish you could see all the children play here in the White House grounds. This coming Saturday afternoon I've agreed to have a great play of hide-and-seek in the White House itself. Wish you were home from school to join in. Do you remember how we all of us used to play hide-and-seek and have obstacle races down the hall at Sagamore Hill with your friends? Last summer I had second thoughts about romping with the children in the old barn, but hadn't the heart to refuse, even though it seems, to put it mildly, rather odd for a stout elderly president to be bouncing over hayricks in a wild effort to get to a goal *before* an active midget of a competitor aged nine years. *(Grins)* However, it was really great fun.

(HE *senses someone—turns—)*

Ah—got you Quentin!

(HE *heaves the pillow across the stage into the wings. After one beat, there is a tinkle of glass!)*

Oh dear.

(HE *grins and comes downstage.)*

Ted: at present I'm acting as peacemaker between the Japanese and the Russians, trying to get the damnable war stopped. Of course, Japan will want to ask more than she ought to ask, and Russia to give less than she ought to give, but there's a chance they'll both prove sensible and make peace.

You know, I enjoy being president, my dear boy. Enjoy the work and having my hand on the lever.

Tonight I think I'm going to enjoy myself more than ever. I'm to be guest speaker at the annual Gridiron Dinner, where I will present, and assume defend, some of my programs. I say "defend," because Mr. J. P. Morgan himself is going to be there. I can hardly wait.

(HE *steps forward into the light that represents the "Gridiron Dinner.")*

So there you have it, gentlemen of the Gridiron Club, in rather brief, bracing form, the goals and proposals of my administration. I thank you for inviting me here tonight, and I certainly thank you for your rapt attention. Now, I said it was rapt attention—but I must say that in certain quarters, particularly over there, at the Speaker's table to my right . . . it seemed to be "wrapped" in rather transparent disapproval. Now now Mr. Morgan, I'm sure that pained expression on your face isn't due to the excellent chicken croquettes.

Now before we're completely asphyxiated by the cigar smoke and embalmed by the brandy, I would like to quote one of Mr. Morgan's brethren, another of American's industrial royalty, Mr. George F. Baer, president of the Reading Railroad. You all know him. Speaking the other day on the divine right of barons—robber, that is—and I think it's a reasonably accurate quote, he said: "The laboring man will be protected and cared for, not by labor agitators, but by the Christian men, to whom God in his wisdom has given control of property interests in this country."

Now I know not of any covenant that Mr. Baer or Mr. Harriman or indeed Mr. Morgan, or any of the rest of you, may have with the Almighty, but I do know I have one with the people of this country, and it is that all of us—every man, woman, and child, Christian or non-Christian, green, black, red, or blue—all of us, not the avaricious self-anointed few, but all of us shall share in the bounty of this land.

I think you'll agree that in the long run the best way to serve any one set of citizens is to try to serve all. The programs I have outlined here tonight are, every one, designed to accomplish just that, and Mr. Morgan, if I may say something to you, sir, from the bottom of my heart—if we are not successful in curtailing your power, then those who come after us shall rise in their righteous wrath and bring not only you—but this whole country to ruin.

I do so pledge.

(TR *stands, angry, dynamic, excited, challenging. The lights change, and* TR *becomes aware of* "EDITH.")

Oh, Edith? No no darling . . . I was . . . just . . . remembering how it was. Thinking. Remembering. Wishing. Hmmmm? They are? The men are back for their answer about the nomination? So soon?

Oh dear, I so wanted to have time to talk to you first. What do you mean it's not necessary? I see. You do hunh . . . you already know my answer. *(Smiles)* Well, then . . . show them in, my dear. Show them in.

Gentlemen. Gentlemen. Good to see you, Bill. Gifford? How are you? *(Looks around, puzzled)* Gentlemen: where is Elihu Root? Oh . . . he's staying with Mr. Taft. *(Lets that sink in for one sad moment)* Well . . . perhaps *we* should stay with Mr. Taft? What . . . thought about it, Bill? Of course I've thought about it. Temptation's great. Danger's greater. But you know, the White House is a bully pulpit, and I must confess . . . I do miss being the weekday preacher.

(HE *grins at them for a long moment)*

My hat is in the ring! Yes—let's go for the nomination.

(With great robust excitement HE *begins to shake hands with all the* "MEN," *when something* "EDITH" *says interrupts.)*

What Edith? Of course, I remember I said the limit of two terms in the White House for any one man was a good principle.

(Pointing to "MENCKEN.")

But remember what Mr. Mencken himself said: "There comes a time in every man's life—when he must *rise above principle!*"

BLACKOUT

ACT TWO

(The stage is empty, the lights dim. After a moment or two, the phone on the desk begins to ring. Two short rings, a pause, two short rings. It repeats this process several times until finally TR*'s voice roars out from offstage:)*

TELEPHONE'S RINGING? WON'T SOMEBODY ANSWER IT? DOESN'T ANYONE HEAR—THAT INFERNAL MACHINE IS CARRYING ON AGAIN!

*(*TR *rushes onstage and up onto the balustrade, in the process of putting on a formal coat.* HE *is getting dressed to go campaigning.)*

Where *is* everybody? Why doesn't—Edie? Loeb? Alice? Boys? Can't you hear—the telephone's ringing! Where are—

*(*HE *looks offstage and sees* "THEM.")

Oh—you're all outside packing the auto—no, no . . . keep at it—we're going to be late for the train anyway—just keep at it all of you . . . I'll get it . . . I'll get it myself.

*(*HE *pulls on his coat and races down the stairs to the desk, glaring at the constantly ringing phone.)*

Alexander Graham Bell should be made to answer the telephone throughout eternity!

*(*HE *picks up the receiver.)*

Hello. Yes, operator. Oh, is that you Marjorie? You the operator on duty? Yes . . . well, no, my dear . . . can't speak now, I'm in a terrible . . . the press? Chicago? Oh . . . all right . . . who? . . . Benedict? All right, fine, put him through, but hurry.

*(*HE *yells into the phone, after all, it's long distance.)*

Hello? Hello? Is that you, Mr. Benedict? What? You're not Benedict? But, I was supposed to speak to a Mr. Benedict. What? Oh, Ben Hecht? *Chicago Journal?* Fine. All right, Mr. Hecht, fine . . . but I really can't talk now . . . what? I can barely hear you, Mr. Hecht. Can you raise your voice. *(Listens)* That's better. *(Shouts)* Can you hear me? *(Listens, nods)* All right, I'll lower mine. *(Listens)* Yes, sir, I will be in Chicago: Tuesday week. That's correct. An interview? Certainly. Yes, the *Journal* has been very kind to me. I welcome your support, sir. Ahhhh . . . well that may be a bit intemperate. It may not be Armageddon, this coming election, but it certainly is an important battle for my party and this country to win. No, sir, no, no. The country certainly cannot afford another four years of Mr. Taft's nonleadership. Very good, Mr. Hecht. Now I really have to go . . . my family is all here, and we're late for—that's your headline for tomorrow? *(Listens)* Yes, I like that. I like that. "The Old Lion Is Back on the Campaign Trail." Bully. Bully. Yes, I feel as lean as a lion . . . and as strong as a bull moose. The fight is on—and I'm stripped to the buff. Yes, of course you can quote me. No, sir . . . not butt: BUFF *(Spells it)* B-U-F-F! I really must go now, young man . . . my family is surrounding me, threatening to carry this person bodily into the auto. Yes, thank you, thank you. Good-bye.

(HE looks over his "FAMILY"—and nods to them.)

All right, my dears, I think I'm all ready. Alice, it was darling of you to come all the way from Washington to see me off.

(HE looks around for last minute, forgotten things, putting them into his various pockets.)

Now, boys, take care of your mother. Edith, take care of the boys, and Ethel, as usual . . . you take care of everybody. What? Oh, yes . . . my hat. Thank you, Quentin.

(HE gets his top hat from the newel-post, puts it carefully on his head, and looks at his "FAMILY," a slow puzzled grin forming on his face.)

What are you . . . laughing at.

(HE follows "THEIR" gaze up to his hat, reaches up to remove the branch of "clematis" that we've seen pinned onto it.)

Oh my dears: clematis. Traveler's joy. Thank you, darlings. Thank you. Of course, you all know that this traveler's joy will always be right here in this house. Well, good-bye my dears . . . I'll write you from Pittsburgh.

(HE rushes around and up the steps, stopping in the center of the balustrade. A soft, loving smile on his face as HE looks down.)

I don't think any of you will ever know how much I love Sagamore Hill.

(There is a slight pause as TR gazes lovingly at his "FAMILY"—then there is the loud roar of a political crowd over the sound system. The lights change, as TR is pulled away from his family and slowly raises his hands to quiet the crowd—the Private Man turning into the Public Man.)

Ladies and gentlemen of the great city of Pittsburgh—my hat *is* in the ring!

(HE laughs and nods as the "CROWD" quiets down—deeelighted to be there. Then begins a "concerto for one politician" in four speeches.)

The fight is on! And I'm stripped to the buff! Of course, I don't want you good people to think I've turned myself into a nudist. I'm really not one of those people who goes about coatless, shirtless—and wears trousers to match!

I simply stand before you wearing only the naked "political" truth. For the first time in the history of our nation two new words have been added to the vocabulary: "direct primaries." Do you know what that means, my friends? It means I can now come and stand before *you* instead of standing in front of those political machine bosses of the Republican Party. It means that instead of being limited merely to choosing between candidates about whose nomination you have nothing to say . . . now *you* can decide whom your candidate for presidency will be. It means you now have the power to break the mold

Bully! Bully! Finis coronet opus, *"The end crowns all!"*

Under the great pines the evening was still with the silence of primeval desolation, and the melancholy of the wilderness came over me like a spell.

A man named Michtom who owned a toy shop over in Brooklyn . . . well, he made a brown plush bear with moveable limbs, button eyes . . . called it Teddy's bear.

I preach not the doctrine of ignoble ease, but the doctrine of the strenuous life.

Here's one from Comrade Gritto . . . one of my Rough Riders: "Dear Colonel . . . I am in trouble. . . . I shot a lady in the eye . . . but I didn't intend to hit the lady. . . . I was shooting at my wife!"

East Side, West Side
All around the town
political clubs are an obscene thing
and socially pull you down.

They're run by horsecar conductors,
saloonkeepers and sellers of pork.
They'll make you a social pariah
on the sidewalks of New York!

I got my first taste of Western life and I loved it . . . felt the beat of hardy life in my veins—the glory of work and the joy of living.

When my heart's dearest died, the light went from my life forever . . . and in that same house . . . on that same day . . . my beloved mother died.

I ran . . . away. Ran . . . West . . . West!

Now look here, Cabot: I can either be President of the United States, or I can control Alice. I can't possibly do both!

My hat is in the ring!

I offer you the ticket to a new era: the era of the Square Deal!

They are stealing my nomination with scandalous disregard for every principle of honesty and decency. This convention no longer represents the Republican Party.

.et history record that at this late :our, on June 22, 1912, a phoenix :as arisen from the ashes: the 'rogressive Party of America!

We stand at Armageddon . . . AND WE BATTLE FOR THE LORRRRRDDDDD!

The instant I received the order, my crowded hour began . . . the Spaniards were shooting down at us . . . on our right was the San Juan Hill . . .

of the political machine, and you can only keep that power by voting for the man with the right ticket. That's the thing that gets you the people admitted to the center of political power which is rightly yours.

I have your ticket to victory—and it is my *record.* I'm running on my record—and if any of you can find a better one . . . I'll run on it! *(Laughs)* But you can't! Just look it over:

Remember the action I took to settle the paralyzing anthracite coal strike of 1902? The arrogant mine owners were brought to heel by strong executive action. Simply told them to negotiate with the miners in good fashion. It was the first time a president stepped in between management and labor—and under threat of federal takeover of the mines—by Godfrey, we got the matter settled!

First and foremost, my concern was to avert a frightful calamity to the country. In the next place I was anxious to save the great coal operators and all the class of big propertied men from the dreadful punishment which their own folly would have brought on them if I had not acted.

Remember when the Great Corporations did their best to kill the bill providing for the Bureau of Corporations? Why those plutocrats sent telegrams and letters to influence various senators and congressmen. Remember how I got hold of one or two of those letters and promptly gave them to the newspapers? Well, as generally happens, the men who were all-powerful as long as they could work in secret—became powerless as soon as they were forced into the open. And the bill went through. I tell you my friends: if any trouble comes from having the light turned on, those corporation rascals have got to remember that it's not really due to the *light*—but to the misconduct it exposes!

Taft is a mollycoddler who kowtows to the machine politicians and the power brokers. I offer you a simple yet powerful program: fair play. Human rights above property rights! When I plead the cause of the crippled brakeman on a railroad, of the overworked girl in a factory, of the stunted child toiling at inhuman labor, of the family dwelling in the squalor of a noisy tenement, of the worn-out farmer in regions where the farms are also worn out. In all these cases I am not only fighting for the weak—I am also fighting for the strong. The sons of all of us will pay in future if we of the present do not do justice in the present. If the fathers cause others to eat bitter bread, the teeth of their own sons shall be set on edge.

I offer you the ticket to a new era: the era of the Square Deal!

*(*TR *moves a little as the roar of the crowd overwhelms him, and cross-fading over this is the sound of a 1912 train*

whistle. The lights change, and the balustrade suddenly looks like the observation platform on the back of a train. TR *waves at the* "CROWD" *below him in greeting. His second speech is a bantering "fugue.")*

Dingo, Dingo! Give me your hand, boy. Good to see you. Deelighted! Watch your horse, there . . . mind the rails; careful, Buck, Chip . . . Durango—so good to see your ugly mugs again. Mind your horses . . . this train gets skittish around them.

Seth! Seth Bullock! Well, by Godfrey, all of Medora must be here. Who's minding the saloons? Who? Hell Roaring Bill Jones? Is that safe, boys? I mean knowing his gargantuan capacity for liquid refreshment . . . what? He got so nervous waiting for me he drank himself under a table. . . . Well, when he comes to, give the old crowbait my love. No, Seth, I can't dismount. Have to ride this iron horse into California by tomorrow. Yes, I'm back in the thick of it again. *(Grins)* Oh my dear old friends, it's so good to be home again, here on the banks of the Little Missouri. The West is a delightful, eternal part of me. Why, there's Hank . . . what'd you say? Will Taft come out here . . . face the people? Well, I rather think that fat old boy follows Aesop's advice . . . that it's easier to be brave from a safe distance! *(To someone else)* What Dingo? Well, I don't know . . . oh . . . all right. Dingo just remembered something my son Kermit once said . . . you all remember Kermit? Brought him out here once when he was a little shaver. Well, Kermit said that his father *(Points to himself)* said: "I never like to go to a wedding or a funeral, because I can't be the bride at the wedding or the corpse at the funeral! Well, it's true you old waddy.

Isn't it better to nominate a man who is used to being at the center of things, than a pussyfooted flubdub like Taft? Our own party leaders didn't realize I was able to hold the Republican Party together and in power only because I insisted on a steady advance and dragged them along with me!

But now the advance has been stopped. The Party and the country are in need of good surgery—and I want to go back into the White House and use the knife and the needle to cut out the disease. Why if Taft goes back he's liable to be more dangerous to the patient than to the disease! *(To someone else)* Yes, I did. That's right, Tracy. Under my interpretation of executive power, yes I did cause many things not previously done to be done. No, I did not usurp power, but I did greatly *(Big grin)* . . . broaden the use of executive power. *(To someone else)* Criticized? 'course I'm criticized. *(With a twinkle)* Men often applaud an imitation ... and hiss the real thing! And by Godfrey, I've been accused of everything, including the sack of Rome and the Great Flood!

Remember how I was accused and criticized when I pushed through the Reclamation Act of 1902? What a hullabaloo from the money boys! Public-land-giveaway they tried to call it! And how they howled about the Pure Food and Drug Act . . . screamed when I stopped the panic of 1907 by executive action concerning the Tennessee Coal and Iron Company. *(Points to somebody)* That's right, Sam ... Northern Securities suit—when I came to office the Sherman Anti-Trust Act was a dead letter. I took it up for the first time and had it enforced. But it's weak weak weak. Needs amending. Needs continued administrative action. Lawsuits against the big trusts're about as practical as a return to the flintlocks of Washington's Continental army! *(To someone else)* I quadrupled the forest reserves, Andy! It's in the record: five national parks. Four big-game refuges. Fifty-one bird reservations. Enacted irrigation laws to turn arid lands into—*(Someone interrupts him)* Fought me, Pete—'course those special interest boys fought me. But I have as little use for them as I do for the man who is always declaiming in favor of an eight-hour day for himself—and doesn't think anything at all of having a sixteen-hour day for his wife!

What's that, Dingo? Taft said he didn't want to fight me for the nomination ... but that "even a *rat* will fight when cornered." Well, boys, I have nothing whatsoever to add to that. *(Grins and shakes his fist.)* You boys here remember better than anybody that I created a Department of Forestry at the Cabinet level to see that all our promises of conservation were kept, but Mr. Taft has welched on the promise. He prefers to ride with the real estate manipulators, the lumber combines, and the railroad barons—the cutthroats who would defile our natural heritage for personal gain. So Mr. Taft, in the name of our children and our children's children, must be pulled from the golden saddle. Conservation means development as much as it means protection. That farmer is a poor creature who skins the land and leaves it worthless to his children. The farmer is a good farmer who, having enabled the land to support him and provide for the education of his children, leaves it to them a little better than he found it himself. I believe the same thing of a nation. That's right, Dutch—I can't deny there're always politicians willing to promise everything to the people, because there're always people who will cheerfully support anybody who promises them an immediate millennium. Well, not only should such politicians be regarded as dishonest and infamous, but the people who're hoodwinked should share the blame. We are honor bound to put into practice what we preach. It's a dreadful thing, boys ... dreadful ... that public sentiment should condone misconduct in a public man;

but this is no excuse for the public man, if by his misconduct he still further degrades the public. Remember: in the last resort no material prosperity, no business acumen, no intellectual development of any kind can atone in the life of a nation for the lack of the fundamental qualities of courage, honesty, and common sense.

Mr. Taft has laid all these basic qualities aside—and he must go.

(HE *makes small movements backwards as if the train is taking off.)*

And so, it seems, must I. We're moving. Watch out for your horses. Give my love at home. So long, boys. Look who's just come late to the party: Hell Roaring Bill Jones . . . how are you? Sober! Good. Stay that way. We need all the votes we can get! All of you—come see me in the White House!

(There is the long whistle of a train, and TR *comes down off the balustrade. As* HE *moves across the stage, the sound of another crowd cross-fades in, the lights change—and* TR *holds up both his hands, grins so his teeth gleam, and begins the third speech of his politician's concerto.)*

Golden golden golden golden! A golden reception from a golden state and a golden city. San Francisco, I salute you! *(To someone)* What friend? Yes, just got in ten minutes ago. How did I come? No no no, didn't use . . . what'd you call it? *(Listens)* No no, didn't use *(Grins)* "Teddy's Ditch!" I just dig them, my friend. Don't need to use them. Remember Little Tommy Tittlemouse? "He caught fishes/in other men's ditches!" Well, we've got our own ditch down in Panama, and we're catching a lot of other countries of the world in it, my friend. *(Grins)* A "ditch" in time, you know.

Me, I bought the right ticket and came Union Pacific this time, across our glorious country. Talked to some other friends of mine along the way . . . let them know I'm back in the fight foursquare. *(Listens to someone)* Yes, sir . . . I do enjoy a good fight, when it's for a good cause. No, sir. Not true. During my seven and a half years in the White House, not one shot was fired against a foreign foe! *(Listens to someone else)* No, sir, wrong again! McKinley took the Philippines. I had to administer it. Hope we did a good job. Tried to teach the Filipinos to respect themselves—and respect us. Key word in foreign relations, my friends:

respect. Without it, no nation can survive. *(Listens to someone else)* Yes. Bully. I like that. Exactly why I sent the battle fleet around the world five years ago. You all saw them here in San Francisco: the great white fleet! Announced to the world that we belonged to *two oceans* now—could move easily from great Pacific to great Atlantic. And as a member of the family of nations, as an equal . . . no more, no less. *(Listens to someone else)* No no no no, I haven't come all the way out here to offer you a patent cure-all. Great Scott, you should distrust whoever pretends to offer you a cure for every ill of the body politic, just as you would a man who offers a medicine which would cure every ill and evil of your individual body! A medicine that's recommended to cure both asthma and a broken leg isn't good for either!

I have come here to say one thing and one thing only: California is a great state, but it is part of a greater nation. Remember, the sands of time are speckled with the dead bones of great nations . . . nations who did not heed the call of the future, who did not expand to the needs of their people. The question today is, will America be such a one? Or will *we,* with courageous leadership that sees the vision and grasps the nettle firmly, continue to be a beacon for all mankind? I know the answer, and I see it in your faces. With proper leadership, it is a resounding—yes!

(There is a roar from the "CROWD," *as* HE *turns and takes a few steps. This fades into the long, low train whistle.* TR *pulls a piece of paper from his inside coat pocket, unfolds it, as the train whistle seems to "blow itself out." The campaign trip comes to an end, and* TR *is about to make his final speech in his politician's concerto.)*

Gentlemen of the New York City Chamber of Commerce *(Glancing at each of them),* Mr. DePew, Mr. Harriman, Mr. Rockefeller, Mr. Rensselaer *(A special glance for his old enemy),* Mr. Morgan . . . and the rest of you honorable gentlemen: I have just completed a six-thousand-mile trip across this great land of ours. In the thirteen primaries held, I won every single state. And even beat Taft in the state of Ohio—his home state. So it appears that if I want it, the Republican Party nomination is mine.

I would now like to share with you some of my observations about this great land—*(*HE *looks up from the paper.)* No sir, I can't do it. Can't do it. *(Holds out the paper)* Gentlemen, I have a rather laboriously prepared speech here outlining my thoughts on the problems of the day, but I can't . . . I mean: with so many of my old acquaintances here . . . so many friends *(Another look over at* MORGAN) and enemies . . . simply can't read to you from a cold piece of paper . . . not going to. *(*HE *crumples the paper in his hand.)* What I want to do is talk to you from my heart.

Many of you men in this room have been most critical of me down through the years . . . to put it mildly. And the sum of all your charges, it seems to me, is that I am a radical. Sometimes it's been in stronger language than that, but "radical" seems to be what you fear. Well, gentlemen, I want to tell you here and now, within the confines of these four walls . . . confidentially . . . that you are one-hundred and fifty percent . . . right!

I am a radical. Feeling as I do about the Declaration of Independence and the Constitution . . . I couldn't be anything else, but . . . and this is a most important "but," I am a radical who wants his radical programs carried out by responsible conservatives. Men like yourselves. Men of wealth. Men of power. Men of knowledge. Men who know, as perhaps no others know, the problems that face our country today. You men could lead the way toward a flowing and prosperous tomorrow. However, first . . . arrogance and brutal indifference toward those less fortunate than we and the base appeal to the spirit of selfish greed, these crippling twin vices must be forever banished if we are to move ahead to an even greater position of power and influence in the world.

We must show by our words, and more importantly by our deeds, that each of us is in very truth his brother's keeper. Gentlemen, it's up to you. The ball is in your court.

*(*HE *gestures with the fist that holds the paper.* HE *looks at it. Holds it out.)*

You mustn't worry about this, gentlemen. It's just my laundry list. *(Grins at* "THEM" *sardonically)* But in the words of an ancient Chinese philosopher: "No tickee, no washee!"

(Blackout.)

(After a moment, a red strip of light appears. Then next to it a white strip of light. Then a blue strip of light.

Then we hear the sounds of the Republican Convention 1912.

Crowds singing: "Hail, hail, the gang's all here!"

Cheering: "We want TEDDY! *We want* TEDDY!"

"TAFT! TAFT! TAFT!"

Finally, a voice cuts through the hullabaloo:

VOICE: *Mr. Chairman? Mr. Chairman? The Great Glorious State of Nebraska votes five delegates for* ROOSEVELT . . . *twenty votes for the next President of the United States,* WILLIAM HOWARD TAFT!

Crowds: TAFT! TAFT! TAFT! TAFT!

We want TEDDY! *We want* TEDDY!

ANOTHER VOICE: *The Magnificent State of Maryland votes three for* ROOSEVELT . . . *eighteen for* TAFT!

*(As the montage continues, it becomes very impressionistic, with "*CROWDS*" screaming for "*TAFT!*" and "We want* TEDDY!*")*

And through this, various voices:

VOICE: *Ten for* ROOSEVELT. *Twenty-six for* TAFT!

VOICE: *Twelve for* ROOSEVELT! *Thirty-five for* TAFT!

SOUNDS OF BOOS, CHEERS: *"Thief! Robbers! Swindlers!"*

Lights come up on the small area of the set that now represents the hotel room. TR *appears, dressed in his long army coat and campaign hat.* HE *is a ball of frustrated, anxious fury. The telephone rings, as the sounds fade out.* TR *answers it.)*

(On phone) Hello, Loeb? Well, where is he? Credentials Committee? Good! Good! That's where he belongs! That's the key to this thing. What? Who am I? Colonel Roosevelt. Just got in. *(Barks)* WHO'RE YOU? Freddie? *(Angry)* Freddie who? Oh, wait, yes . . . yes . . . I remember you, Freddie. It's all right son. Didn't mean to frighten—what? What do you mean, "What's going on"? You're down on the floor and I'm up here in a hotel room! No no, it's all right, son. I know what's going on. I'll tell you what's going on: it's a case of good old-fashioned political rape. But they're not going to get away with it. Do you hear that, son? We're going to lick 'em, my boy. Going to lick 'em. Now, you stay at your post.

(Somebody enters)

Yes, Bill, good you brought the tally sheets. What? *(Listens to Bill, then quickly to the phone)* Hello, son. Freddie? Who's there with you? Put him on. *(Waits)* Hello, Senator. Bill White tells me some of our people are threatening to walk out of the hall because of this credentials mess. I know Loeb's over there, but I want you to tell our people to stand firm. We're going to lick the machine on its own ground. No, look Senator. We have the votes! We've got them! We got the delegates in the primaries. . . . *(Listens)* I know Credentials is stacked for Taft, but there has to be some honor among those thieves! *(Nods)* Oh . . . and Senator, tell La Follette now is the time to declare for me. He was just a stalking horse, anyway. Fine.

(Hangs up)

Kermit, let me have those tally sheets.

(Looks them over, picking out names)

Bill, I want you to get over to Credentials. Talk to Coombs, Russel, and James Bennett. I don't care if they're Taft's corset-lacers! Get to them! They used to be honorable men!

(Phone rings. HE *answers.)*

Colonel Roosevelt. *(Listens)* Yes, Loeb . . . yes . . . 252 contested delegate seats? Great Scott! *(Listens)* What do you mean there may be some slippage? They can't take a one of them away from us . . . all right, get back over there and let me know immediately. *(Listens)* Who? Yes, put him on . . . hello, Gifford? Yes, just got in. La Follette refuses to declare for me? Why? *(Nods knowingly)* The machine rolleth on! *(Listens)* What do you mean, we're falling apart? California? We have *all* of California! Ryan? Why that miserable, mealy-mouthed little worm! You get over to his delegation and you tell him his sacred honor is at stake . . . to say nothing of his future in Republican politics. And if that doesn't work, tell him I'll come over personally . . . and shoot him!

*(*HE *hangs up.)*

(Somebody comes in) Yes, Ted? What is it? Spit it out, boy. *(Repeating)* The South has gone to Taft? Gutless, gutless, gutless.

(Phone rings. HE *answers.)*

Colonel Roosevelt! Yes, Loeb. Calm down, Bill. Calm down. Now say that again, and slowly. What's the matter . . . are you crying? Slowly . . . slowly now. *(Repeats)* Of the 252 contested delegate seats . . . 238 seated for Taft? I don't believe it. I—

*(*HE *simply stares unbelieving for a moment.)*

(To phone) No, Bill, I'm all right. No . . . no . . . no further orders.

*(*HE *hangs up.)*

(To others in the hotel room) Well, gentlemen, thirteen states, thirteen primaries . . . we won 273 to Taft's 46. And now the machine is stealing every one! The cause of our opponents has now become nakedly clear. It is the cause of the political bosses and special privilege. They are stealing my nomination with scandalous disregard for every principle of honesty and decency. This convention no longer represents the Republican Party. All of you, get over to the hall. Get out on the floor. Tell everyone who was elected by the people as a Roosevelt candidate not to vote on anything at all, and to await further orders.

*(Notices "*GIFFORD PINCHOT*")* Yes, Gifford, come in. What is it? They offer a compromise. *(Stands straight and firm)* We will not compromise with thieves! There will be no compromise!

(There is the sound of a large cheering mob. TR *turns and marches up to the balustrade to stand framed by the two big elephant tusks, bathed in a golden light. In the thick of battle,* HE *raises his arms in a lordly way to silence the mob.)*

In another part of this city tonight, at this very moment, the Republican Party is ruthlessly betraying the trust of the rank and file . . . the people. They have compelled us to forge a new party. A new instrument of government responsive to the people. Let history record that at this late hour, on June 22, 1912, a phoenix has arisen from the ashes: the Progressive Party of America!

(Another roaring cheer, which TR *diminishes by raising his arms.)*

I proudly accept your nomination. And here is my confession-of-faith: what happens to me is of no consequence. I am to be used, as in a doubtful battle any man is used, to his hurt or not, so long as he is useful; and then cast aside and left to die. I wish you to feel this. I shall need no sympathy when you are through with me. We fight in honorable fashion for the good of mankind . . . fearless of the future . . . unheeding of our individual fates . . . with unflinching hearts and undimmed eyes . . . we stand at Armageddon . . . AND WE BATTLE FOR THE LORRRRRRDDDDDDD!

*(The "*CROWD*" roars its approval. The light is even more golden and glowing as the "*CROWD*" bursts into song: "The Battle Hymn of the Republic" intertwined with "Onward Christian Soldiers."*

TR *moves with a pleased, "majestic" smile—off the balustrade and strides across the stage listening to the glorious voices.*

Then HE *looks up to "*MENCKEN.*" With one hand he silences the singing, which fades into the distant background. With the other hand he beckons to "*MENCKEN*":)*

Mencken, come on down. For once in your life come down into the arena and join us. It's going to be a glorious fight, man. What's that? Tyranny of the majority? Read your history, boy—the only tyrannies are the tyrannies of the *minorities:* the tyrannies of power, the tyrannies of money, the tyrannies of royalty, the tyranny of the trust, the railroads . . . Oh Mencken, the ship of privilege is ready to sink, and you of all people should be glad I'm here to give it the coup de grâce. *(Listens)* What? Still the demagogue . . . oh we've been through that, Mencken. A game? What? A child? I should remember that I'm always six years old? Very well, Mencken. So be it. So be it! Then a little child shall lead them.

(HE turns and walks across the stage toward the other side, smashing one fist into the palm of the other hand to emphasize each point:)

Lead them to social justice. Lead them to a minimum wage. Lead them to a guaranteed eight-hour day. A guaranteed vote for women! Guaranteed end to child labor! Guaranteed recall of all elected officials, including judges—

(When TR reaches the side of the stage, there is a sudden, startling flash of gunpowder and a frightening, loud gunshot.

HE sucks in his breath and is thrown backwards to the ground.

A strobe light is on, so TR moves as if in slow motion, as HE gets slowly to his feet, gasping and staggering.)

No, no . . . don't hurt him. Don't . . . don't . . . don't kill him. Bring him to me. There's . . . always a lunatic fringe . . . on the skirts of every reform movement. Poor creature . . . take him away. Don't hurt him . . . don't hurt . . . leave me . . . no . . . let . . . I'm not going anywhere . . . I have this speech . . . and I'm going to deliver it.

(Staggers across the stage.)

(To audience) My friends . . . I'm going . . . ask you to be very quiet. Don't know if you fully understand . . . but I have been shot. Please . . . it takes more than that . . . to kill . . . a bull moose.

Bullet . . . is in me now . . . I have . . . message to deliver . . . and I will deliver it . . . as long as there is life in my body. Now friends . . . friends . . . understand I am ahead of the game anyway. No man has had a . . . happier life . . . give you my word . . . don't give a rap for being shot. Don't waste sympathy on me. I don't need your sympathy . . . I need you to vote the Progressive Party ticket. If one soldier who carries the flag is down, another will take it from his hands . . . always. The army is true . . . if the cause is true.

(HE *makes one long rasping gasp for air, and the lights black out.*
There is a pause.
Then the lights come up again, and HE *is standing there. Straighter.)*

I survived the bullet, but lost the war. The Democrats won, with a college professor named Woodrow Wilson. I beat Taft, but it was small consolation. The country was not in a principled or heroic mood. I think the American people were a little tired of me. *(Small smile)* A feeling with which I cordially sympathized.

(HE *moves slowly to the coatrack. Hangs up his hat and removes his army great-coat.* HE *hangs that up and gets an "old sweater," which* HE *puts on and buttons up.)*

I ran away again. This time to the jungles of the Amazon. Took Kermit with me, and at the request of the Brazilian government, we charted one-thousand miles of unknown wilderness river. The Brazilian government showed its appreciation by giving the cartographers a name for the blank space on the map: Rio Teodoro. Almost didn't make it. I crushed my leg against a rock in the rapids, and then when malaria struck me . . . well, the infection and the fever made me a terrible burden. . . . I urged the others to push on without me . . . no man has the right to go on an exploration unless he will refuse to jeopardize the welfare of others. His duty is to go forward until he drops. I . . . had . . . secretly determined to kill myself . . . but . . . blessed Kermit took command . . . and they carried me through. I overmatched myself . . . again. I suppose the whole thing was foolhardy for a man of my years, but I had to go. *(Wistfully)* It was my last chance to be a boy.

(HE *"limps" now, as the lights come up*

and he moves into his armchair in the "North Room.")

Edie and I had a glorious three-hour ride yesterday. Then, in the evening, we sat here in the North Room before the blazing fire and watched a snowstorm gradually turn into a blizzard. I felt as though I were finally going into hibernation, which is right . . . only natural . . . I suppose.

Good news from Groton on Quentin's grades. Heavens! To think one of our family standing as high as that. It's almost paralyzing.

All the children are each in his or her own particular sphere, doing what they ought to do. Seem to be happy, and yet behaving themselves. As am I. As am I. Enjoying myself mightily.

(HE *isn't, of course. And his restlessness brings him out of the chair and onto his feet, while he tries to enumerate all the things he "enjoys" as* HE *limps across the stage to the desk.)*

Passions long deferred can now, at last, be fully embraced: wildlife sanctuaries, not nearly enough of 'em. And the ones we have are badly administered. That's a fight worth fighting.

And the nature fakers. Must join that fight again. You know about the "nature fakers"? Those are the so-called natural scientists who attribute human traits to wild animals . . . a great disservice to both species! Well, my heavens . . . it's a terrible thing . . . to make a youngster grow up believing a chipmunk thinks like his sister!

The Boy Scout movement. Must pick that up again. Marvelous movement: teaches boys to be self-reliant . . . appreciate nature and life in the rough.

Now that's another thing, something else that's a deferred passion of mine: simplification of the English language. Did you hear that word *rough*—it should really be spelled r-u-f. Ruff! Or at least r-u-f-f! When I was president, I tried to get legislation through the Congress to simplify over 300 words in our language. But Congress raised such a linguistic cackle, I withdrew the egg. Maybe I could get it hatched now. Worthwhile project . . . worthwhile.

And of course, there's always my books . . . my writing. So much to do. *(Big sad sigh)* So much to do.

(HE *sits for a moment, staring at his desk, his hands nervously drumming. A sad "old man" with nothing "important" to do.)*

(Suddenly, HE *is interrupted by* "EDITH.")

Oh, Edie? Come in . . . come in . . . no no, dear . . . you're not interrupting anything . . . vital. Oh, we can dine anytime, my dear. Any time will do. Why, of course, I'm all right. Just . . . making a battle plan. There's so much to be done, but I just can't seem to get at it.

What? Read to you after dinner? Well, why wait . . . I'll read to you right now. Be deeelighted. No no no . . . this can wait.

(Dismisses the desk with a gesture)

This can wait.

(HE *gets up as quickly as* HE *can, limps over to the table and two armchairs.* SHE *is "sitting" in one of the chairs.)*

What would you like me to read to you?

(Finds a book among several)

Ah. *Electra.* New translation by George Gilbert A. Murray. Just read it. Seems to me he's rendered the play admirably. First twenty lines are particularly good . . . probably because they match my own interpretation of the original.

(Pounds the book)

What extraordinary people the Greeks were, my dear. I don't know whether to admire most the wonderful power and artistic beauty of the play, or to shrink from the revolting nature of the theme. Well well well, I've never been able to see that there was the slightest warrant for resenting the death of Agamemnon on the part of his son and daughter, to whose loss the brother and sister never even allude. Not to mention the fact that he got possession of the daughter by treachery in order to slay her! And that he brought Cassandra home with him as his mistress. No no, Edie—I think Clytemnestra's sin mild indeed compared with Agamemnon's! I mean if, as it's said, the Greek judgment was influenced by the very different culpabilities to be attached to a man and a woman, then why should no punishment whatever be awarded to Electra for her part in the murder of her mother, in which she was really the determining factor. *(Little mad)* Whereas Orestes was haunted by the Furies, Electra was promptly married "to an earl who kept his carriage"!

Hmmm? You don't want me to read *Electra. (Puts down the book, to look for another.)* All right, my dear . . . how about some . . . *(Holds up a book)* Gobineau's *Inégalité des Races Humaines?* No no, well-written book . . . contains some good guesses . . . but for a student to approach it for serious information . . . would be much as if an albatross should apply to a dodo for an essay on flight. *(Puts it down)* Maybe we should dip into the Pigskin Library: some Spencer . . . Macaulay, the essays? Or . . . or Dante . . . we haven't done Dante together for some time. . . . I have Carlyle's translation of the Infern—well, how about Braithwaite's *Book of Elizabethan Verse?* Then, maybe some Owen Wister? Irwin? Who is—*(Gets the book* SHE *wants him to read)* Oh, Edie, are you sure you want me to read this—Of course I remember him, dear. . . . He's the fellow wrote that silly doggerel about my peacemaking efforts in the Russian-Japanese War. But why in heaven's name would you want me to read—all right, my dear. If you insist. If you insist.

*(*HE *limps over to sit in his armchair, as* HE *begins to read.)*

Tis morning, and King Theodore
Upon his throne sits he,
As blithely as a king can sit,
Within a free countree.

*(*HE *sits, but makes a funny, sour face at the poem. Glances at "*EDITH.*" Goes on.)*

And now he thinks of submarines,
And now of peace and war,
His royal robe he handeth Loeb
Then wireth to the Czar:

"Come off, come off, thou great
white Czar,
Come off thy horse so high,
Send envoys straight and arbitrate
The diplomatic pie."

(HE grimaces to himself.)

Then straightway to the "Mickadoo"
This letter he doth limn:
"Come off thy perch, thou morning sun,
And do the same as him."

Edith do you really want me to read this ridiculous thing?

Well, my dear, I didn't find it amusing then, and I must say I still don't find it amusing. After all, Edith, that was rather serious business. I stopped the war and I stopped the killing.

But yes yes, I suppose there were certain comic elements. There's always something comic about all the diplomatic folderol, isn't there? I think really, Edith, the funny thing here was that the Russians . . . were so tall . . . and the Japanese . . . were so very small. And I was in the middle in more ways than one.

Oh yes, my dear, the banquet on the presidential yacht. *(Laughs)* How could I ever forget it. . . .

(HE puts down the book, and gets up to "play it out for us.")

Why it was right here in our front yard, Edith, right out there on the bay. And you know, my dear, I think that's what did it, finally. That banquet sealed the peace.

Oh, you were furious with me, remember? One of the few times. You said as hostess, you wouldn't allow it, but that was before you understood the real problem.

(With an amused sigh)

Remember Sergei, that giant bearded Count . . . six feet four if he was an inch. Mother Russia was in his voice as he intoned:

(Imitates SERGEI)

Mr. Roosevelt, the Minister of
the Czar will be seated first
. . . before the Japanese.

And then there was tiny Komura. Dear Jutaro.

(Imitates KOMURA)

Mr. President, this unworthy
emissary of the Mikado will
of course be seated *before*
the Russians.

And both of 'em had to be in the seat of honor at my right. In one chair. I'll never forget their faces, Edie, when we entered the banquet hall . . .

(HE *steps into the banquet hall and looks at the* MEN *on either side of him with a cunning grin, then to the audience.)*

No chairs!

(HE *laughs uproariously at the memory.)*

It's an old American custom, gentlemen. We call it buffet! *(Laughs again)* Eat standing up! Good for the digestion.

And it turned out to be good for the world's digestion, Edie. I think they got the point: diplomatic games being played with people's lives. And near the end, when I got them to shake hands.

(His right hand becomes the tiny hand of the Japanese.)

Jutaro's delicate little hand.

(His left hand becomes a giant paw, as it descends on the other.)

And Sergei's enormous paw . . . joining together.

(THEY *shake, and* HE *glows.)*

All the rest, the meetings in Portsmouth, the treaty ceremony, my Nobel Peace Prize—none of it could ever compare to that one moment of human civility and reason.

By George, it was bully! Just bully.

(HE *stares with great glow at his joined hands, until* "EDITH" *interrupts.)*

What? Oh, Edie, come on . . . you don't want me to really read the final stanza. All right. All right, my dear . . . just the last stanza.

(HE *goes back to get the book and reads quickly to get it done.)*

And now when ancient grandsires sit
Within the evening's gray,
And oysters frolic noisily
All over Oyster Bay,
The Graybeard tells his little niece
How Theodore did trek
To drag the gentle bird of peace
To Portsmouth . . . by the neck.

(HE *stares at the page, and grins at it.)* Well, that's cleverer than I thought! And you're clever too, my dear. Don't think I didn't know what you were doing—trying to make the old boy realize his life hasn't been a total waste. You're right, Edie. Time to do a little more "remembering" at my age . . . before I start settling in for good. Well, now we can get rid of Mr. Irwin, right?

(Tosses down the book)

Now how about reading Owen Wister? *(Listens, frowns)* Henry James? You wouldn't do that to me . . . you would. Let's compromise, Edie—Shakespeare. Good. Macbeth? Too bloody. Hamlet? Oh no, Edith, you . . . don't—

(Gets up to get the book)

No, it's all right, dear. I'll read Hamlet. It's my fault. . . . I just have never been able to understand that young man's vacillation.

(Suddenly HE *hears something. Stops. Serious. Cautious.)*

Shhhhh. Listen, Edie, listen. *(Listens)* Crack of thunder? No. No. That's cannon fire . . . coming closer. *(Listens)* Wait. A gunshot. Sarajevo! What I told them was going to happen—is happening. The Kaiser is marching. *(A roaring, wistful whisper)* Ohhhhh Lord how I would like to be president now.

(Lights become more focused, so TR *is*

trapped in a spotlight that follows him around.)

Listen. Quiet. Nothing. Silence. Wilson . . . says nothing. *(Nervously puzzled)* How can . . . how can Wilson be silent? *We should go in. (Listens)* Shhhhh. Shhhhh. Ohhhhh . . . voices . . . screams . . . crying . . . women . . . children . . . voices . . . screaming . . . crying . . . scream— *(Puts his hands to his ears to stop the terrible noise)* Ohhhhh. The *Lusitania* sunk! Men, women, children murdered. Our own fellow countrymen . . . murdered on the high seas. Innocent. We're at war! Why doesn't Wilson say something. *(Listens)* Wait a minute . . . he's speaking. Wilson says: "a nation may be *(With shocked amazement)* . . . too *proud* to fight?"

*(*TR *begins a slow, restless pacing which grows faster and more intense as the scene continues, as* HE *talks to the various members of his* "FAMILY.")

Did you hear that, Kermit? The man is incredible! And so is his Secretary of State, William Jennings Bryan: that professional yodeler . . . that human trombone! Prize jacks, both of 'em . . . peace at any price, universal arbitrationists!

No, no, Quenty, you can't arbitrate with bullies! Sooner or later you must stand and fight or die . . . and the sooner the better!

No, Ted, if Germany smashes England, our turn will be next. Yes, I know what Wilson says, but political neutrality not based on moral reasons is no more admirable than the neutrality of Pontius Pilate!

That's it, Quenty-quee. Well put. Boys, did you hear what Quentin said. We can never wash our hands of the truth. It's indelible . . . the eternal damned spot . . . won't go away until the people face it squarely: *we are at war!*

Yes yes, I know boys, I tried to tell them: twenty-four cities in two years, and God knows how many luncheons and Rotary Club dinners . . . everywhere they'd listen to me. But now, boys, your father must seem a truculent, bloodthirsty warrior, carefully trying to thwart the humane plan of the "noble" Mr. Wilson. Oh yes, Kermit, he has a "plan": to bring universal peace by writing exquisitely phrased letters. I wonder how many admonitory notes he's sent to the Kaiser so far. I lost count after 11,675, Series B!

Boys, Woodrow Wilson is a glowing example of everything you must never become . . . tricky and false, without one spark of loftiness in him, without one touch of the heroic in his cold, timid soul!

(To the audience)

Mr. Wilson now "dwells" at the summer White House in Shadow Lawn. Well, there should be shadows enough at Shadow Lawn: the shadows of men, women, and children who have risen from the ooze of the ocean bottom; the shadows of the helpless Mr. Wilson didn't dare protect, less he might have to face danger. Shadows of deeds that were never done, shadows of lofty words, followed by no action—intellectual debauchery. Shadows of the tortured dead. Those are the shadows proper for Shadow Lawn.

(In a great rush of anger, TR *turns away. Then* HE *hears something else.)*

Listen. Wilson is speaking . . . yes . . . yes . . . yes . . . YESSSSSSS!

(Sound of the song "Over There" starts softly and keeps building louder and louder.)

(Ecstatic and almost shouting) That's what I've been shouting all along! When men finally have to pay heed to a prophecy, they relieve themselves by stoning the prophet. But this prophet doesn't give a hang! We're in it! Two years late . . . but by Godfrey—we're finally in the war . . . *(One long roar)* AND IT'S BULLYYYYYYYYY!

(Sound of the song roars out as loud as possible—"Over There"!

TR *marches up to the coatrack, puts on his army greatcoat and his campaign hat. Marches downstage to face the desk, which is now "*WILSON*'s office."* TR *slaps his feet together in crisp military attention, salutes, and folds his arms behind him in "parade rest" position. Music is out.)*

Mr. President, Colonel Theodore Roosevelt at your disposal. Thank you, sir.

*(*HE *relaxes, and pulls a paper out of his inside coat pocket, as* HE *talks to "*WILSON*," who has risen and moved out from behind the desk.)*

Mr. Wilson, as you've no doubt heard, a rather extraordinary number of men have rallied behind me, and I stand ready—at your direction of course—to lead them as a voluntary regiment to France as soon as possible. Oh, you hadn't heard? Well, it's been in all the papers, and I thought . . . yes, sir, these are, of course, busy times for all of us.

Well, I'm grateful for your interest in the idea. Now here is what—

(WILSON *has interrupted.*)

My wife. She's lovely as ever, thank you. And Mrs. Wilson? Good. Now this is what I propose—

(WILSON *interrupts and moves to another part of the stage.*)

My children? All well, thank you. In fact, the boys are all in the fight save one: Ted's in the army. Archie too. Kermit's been with the British for some time, and Quentin will be in the Air Force shortly. Thank you sir; I must confess that I'm grateful to have four such sons.

(HE *holds out the paper, pointing to it.*)

I have here, Mr. President, the T.O. for the regi—*(Pointedly)* Table of Organization, sir. I believe it's all in order: *(Rattles off points on the paper)* All necessary expenses will be derived from private funds. Staff officers all approved. Quartermaster approved. Weaponry approved. Commissary approved. Transport and supplies approved. *(Listens)* Why, by *me,* of course . . . and the secretary of war. Baker's an old friend of mine. Did some good work for me in the past.

("WILSON" *has moved back to his desk. So* TR *is forced to follow him.)*

Now all that remains is for you to give . . . well, time is of the essence. I felt it imperative to move with dispatch. Let the Germans and our allies know that even though we were criminally unprepared, we are indeed coming over.

("WILSON" *moves away from the desk.* TR *in his anxiety moves behind the desk.)*

And for our own people, too, this regiment of volunteers should galvanize the entire country. Just give me your hand on it, Mr. President. I'll announce it to the press right now, I've got them waiting outside.

("WILSON" says something that makes TR realize that he is "occupying" the president's desk.)

Oh . . . excuse me, sir.

(HE backs away, as "WILSON" comes over to sit behind the desk once more.)

Now wait . . . hold on . . . I may have acted hastily, but certainly with no ulterior motive. I see. *(Deep controlled breath)* Wilson, I came here because I firmly believed that an ex-president of the United States leading the first American soldiers into combat would electrify this country and the world—and scare the hell out of the Hun!

(Quietly, passionately) Mr. President, please, let me be of service to my country by dying in some reasonable, honorable fashion . . . at the head of my regiment in France.

(HE waits and then seems to sink into himself. Slowly he leaves the desk and walks out of the scene, slowly limping his way back to his armchair in the North Room of Sagamore Hill. He slumps into the chair. Staring.)

Yes. Yes, Edie. Mr. Wilson gave me some time.
Turned me down. Turned me down.
Hmmmm? Oh, yes . . . the overcoat.

(With great worn-out effort HE stands and removes his coat.)

Is my cross of silk still in place, my dear? My Siegfried's cross? It is? Good. Good. Good good good.

(HE hangs up his hat and coat, and is in his old sweater once again looking old and tired.)

Well I'm out of it . . . out of it . . . out of it.
(To "EDIE" who's standing now) Yes, dear. I'll see you at dinner. I'm just going to write a letter to Kermit first.

(HE nods her out of the room. Gets his

pen and writing pad. Sits to write his letter.)

Dearest Kermit: turned sixty today. And I'm glad. Somehow it gives me the right to be titularly old as I feel. Huzzah! Quentin is in! Off to become part of the new Air Force. Mother said it was hard when the youngest went, but you can't bring up boys to be eagles and expect them to turn out sparrows. Early this morning the newspapermen told us Archie had been given the Croix de Guerre. Then we received Ted's cable saying Archie had been wounded. At lunch, we filled our glasses with Madeira and drank them off to Archie. Mother, eyes shining, cheeks flushed, as pretty as a picture and as spirited as any heroine of romance, dashed her glass on the floor, shivering it into pieces, saying: "that glass will never be drunk out of again!"

Here the woods are showing green foam and the gay yellow of forsythia has appeared. I've ceased to fret at my impotence to do anything in this great crisis. I putter around like the other old frumps, trying to help with Liberty Loans, Red Cross and the like.

I rejoice that my four sons are playing parts in the greatest of the world's greatest days. What man of gallant spirit doesn't envy you. You have seized the great chance, as it was seized by those who fought at Gettysburg, Agincourt, and Marathon. You are having your crowded hours . . . and I am beside you all . . . in spirit. With great love. The . . . old . . . frump.

(TR *looks at his letter for a moment. Then* HE *glances up at "*MENCKEN.*"* HE *gets out of the armchair and gets his campaign hat.*

HE *puts it on and limps over to the desk, with another glance at "*MENCKEN.*"*

TR *sits behind the desk, puts down the writing pad. Looks again at "*MENCKEN.*" Decides to open the desk drawer. From it he removes a pistol.* HE *expertly checks the barrel to make sure it's loaded. Satisfied, he slams the drawer shut. Then with one more look at "*MENCKEN,*" he gets up—picks up a "telegram" from the desk, and limps around to where he can face "*MENCKEN*" with the gun in one hand and the telegram in the other.)*

Mencken? What do you think? From Captain Jinks to Old Frump.
What's the matter, Mencken, are you too overcome with emotion? Can't speak? I have something I want to read to you.

(Listens, looks for "MENCKEN")

Well, he's . . . gone. Walked out on me. Hmmmmp.

(Decides to read the telegram to the audience)

"This afternoon, at 2:45 P.M., Lieutenant Quentin Roosevelt brought down his first German airplane over France." Needless to say, Mrs. Roosevelt and I are as proud as peacocks.

(HE folds up the telegram, puts it into his sweater pocket, the lights change, as HE kneels laboriously. An old man, playing out his own "crowded hour" in Cuba.)

The instant I received the order, *my* crowded hour began. The Spaniards were shooting down at us, low-grazing fire from the top of the hill. I formed my men in skirmishes. On our right was the San Juan River. On the left, a sunken road. They were crouched, or lying prone, waiting for my command. I had intended to go into action on foot, but on horseback I could see the men better . . . and they could see me.

(A spotlight pins down TR as HE "mounts" his horse for troop inspection, "riding" down the line of men slowly.)

There was Dudley Dean, quarterback, Harvard.
Bob Wren, another quarterback. Tennis champion.
Yale men: Wall. The high jumpers: Garrison and Girard.
Princeton men: Devereaux . . . Changing. Footballers. Lannard, tennis champion.
Bucky O'Neill, gunfighter, mayor of Prescott, Arizona.
Smoky Moore, the broncobuster.
Pollack, full-blooded Pawnee.
Colbert, Chickasaw.
Adair, Holderman—both Cherokees.
College men, noncollege men, Catholics, Jews, Protestants. Soon many of them would be buried in a common grave . . . as Americans.

(HE has reached the end of the line of men.)

Always in that split second before an advance, there seems to be a moment when everything stops. For that instant, all breathing seems to stop. Your mind is a blank . . . and the only movement . . . the pounding of your heart.

(To the "MEN")

All right, men. Move out . . . slowly. Keep your interval and stay low.

(To the audience)

Always there is that hesitation, each man looking to see whether the other will go first. And then . . . slowly . . . they move—

(HE looks down)

Come on, son. Move forward. Son? Are you afraid? Son?

(TR "dismounts." Kneels to help the boy.)

(To audience)

He was dead.
A bullet had gone through him . . . lengthwise.
I, exposed on horseback, had been spared. He, under cover . . . had been killed.

(HE turns and moves upstage to crouch behind a log.)

The men had picked their way slowly to a low wall at the base of the hill. The enemy fire had been deadly, and now increased in volume. Ahead, rose a treeless slope, leading to a blockhouse . . . and the top . . . a million miles away.

(After a moment, TR rises up. And a low moanlike sound comes from him that grows into a loud and roaring command:)

CHARRRRRRRGEEEEEEE!

(The lights illuminate the desk, which is now "San Juan Hill."

Sound: Rifle fire and ricocheting bullets. A Gatling gun.

Music: A piano plays very slowly, "Hot Time in the Old Town Tonight."

TR *walks in almost slow motion toward the desk, his gun in front of him. The music tempo increases, as his walk increases. Until* HE *climbs a chest and up to the top of "San Juan Hill," which is the desk.* HE *fires his revolver.)*

I GOT ONE! I GOT ONE!

*(*HE *continues to fire, until something he hears makes him turn—look—and freeze. Music and sound are out abruptly.*

TR *stands frozen for a moment on top of San Juan Hill. His face startled. Hurt. Suddenly, the gun seems to burn his hand—he throws it down.)*

(A low, awful moan)

Oh my God . . . Quentin shot down! QUENTIN KILLED. QUENTIN WAS KILLED. Oh my god . . . not Quentin . . . not Quenty-quee . . . oh my God.

(His body slumps, HE *is sobbing. Looking very old. An old man, standing on a desk.)*

Cold . . . feel . . . so cold . . . cold. Not Quentin. Oh my God, not Quentin.

*(*HE *collapses to his knees, then is able to slide himself off the desk to sit for a moment in the chair, crying now, his head on the desk.)*

Not . . . to touch him . . . anymore . . . not to . . . smell him . . . feel his fine glowing mind . . . Quentin . . . so many things . . . we haven't talked about . . . so many . . . oh my God.

(The phone rings. Jarringly. HE *just stares at it. Crying. Slowly jerks the receiver off the hook. Puts it to his ear.)*

Colonel Roosevelt. The . . . press? Statement? No, I have . . . wait . . . wait . . . Quentin's mother and I are proud he had a chance . . . to render . . . some service . . . to his country.

*(*HE *nods at the phone. Hangs up. And then says:)*

Good-bye. Ohhhhh, Quentin. I feel as though I was a hundred years old and had never been young.

(Slowly, this broken old man stands up, and with some confusion decides to go out of the room. But HE *notices a Teddy bear on a table. Goes to get it. Looks at it, then tenderly hugs it to his chest. Hurt and crying. Then,* TR *comes forward to face the audience.)*

Only those are fit to live who do not fear to die. None is fit to die who shrinks from the joy of life . . . and the duty of life. For life and death are both parts of the same Great Adventure.

(With great reverence)

And . . . it's bully.

(With whispered defiance)

Just bully!

*(*HE *looks once more at the Teddy bear. Then he kisses it, and with glowing tears in his voice,* HE *says:)*

Look sharp!

(HE throws the Teddy bear into the audience: "Passing the torch from one generation to the next" (as HE wrote)—or maybe just reaffirming some joy-of-life.)

(Then, TR turns and walks upstage and through the portals, disappearing into the infinity of his artifacts.
AS THE LIGHTS FADE OUT.)

THE END

THEODORE ROOSEVELT (1858-1919)

1858 October 27, Theodore Roosevelt, Jr., born at parental home, 28 East 20th Street, New York City.

1873 After private tuition, Theodore begins preparation for his college education at the Cutler School, New York City.

1876 Young Theodore enters Harvard.

1878 October 18, first meeting between Theodore and Alice Hathaway Lee of Chestnut Hill, Massachusetts.

1880 Theodore graduates from Harvard and prepares to study law at Columbia University. October 27, Theodore Roosevelt marries Alice Hathaway Lee.

1882 Theodore, disillusioned with the Law, abandons his studies and is elected to the New York State Legislature.

1884 February 12, a daughter is born to Alice and Theodore Roosevelt. She is named Alice Lee.
February 14, double tragedy strikes the Roosevelt residence at 6 West 57th Street in New York City. In the early morning hours, Martha Bulloch Roosevelt, Theodore's mother, dies. Shortly after noon, Alice Hathaway Lee Roosevelt, Theodore's wife, dies. Teddy, overcome by grief and ill health, leaves the East and settles in North Dakota, taking up the life of a cattle rancher.

1885 Theodore Roosevelt completes his home, Sagamore Hill.

1886 Teddy Roosevelt returns to the East, and runs unsuccessfully for Mayor of New York City.
December 2, marries Edith Kermit Carow in London.
Spends next three years pursuing literary and historical work.

1889 Appointed by President Harrison as member of the Civil Service Commission in Washington, D.C. (annual salary $3,500). Soon becomes its President and so conducts the Commission's business that it becomes one of the most important Government offices. Theodore Roosevelt achieves national prominence by serving on the Commission until 1895.

1894 W. L. Strong is elected Mayor of New York City. He asks Theodore Roosevelt to become Police Commissioner.

1895 Mayor Strong inaugurated; Teddy Roosevelt becomes New York's Police Commissioner (until 1897). He completely reorganizes the Department, making it one of the most efficient Departments in the country; he breaks a long existing system of Police graft, yet gains the goodwill and admiration of the rank and file.

1897 April 19, President McKinley nominates T.R. Assistant Secretary of the Navy.

1898 May 10, resigns position to become Lieutenant-Colonel of the First U.S. Volunteer Cavalry—popularly called the "Rough Riders."

May 11, Rough Riders land in Cuba. Roosevelt's unorthodox military exploits, especially his impetuous charge up Kettle Hill (San Juan), make him a hero.

September 27, returning from the Spanish-American War, T.R. is nominated as the Republican Gubernatorial candidate.

November 8, T.R. is elected by a majority of 20,000 votes.

1899 January 2, T.R. takes oath of office as Governor of New York. Among his accomplishments during the two years he serves is a new Civil Service Law, and a revision of the Tenement House Law.

1900 T.R. refuses nomination to second term as Governor.

June 21, nominated at Republican Convention as Vice-Presidential candidate in McKinley's second term.

November 13, McKinley and Roosevelt are elected with 849,000 plurality.

1901 March 4, T.R. takes office as Vice-President.

September 14, upon the assassination of President McKinley in Buffalo, N.Y. Theodore Roosevelt is sworn in as the 26th President, the youngest man ever to reach that office, 42 years, 10 months, 18 days. As President, T.R. fights corruption of politics by big business, vigorously uses the Sherman Anti-Trust Law to oppose giant corporations, intervenes in coal strike on behalf of the public, threatening to send the Army into the mines, to keep the people from freezing. He institutes the Department of Commerce and Labor, obtains laws to forbid rebates to favored corporations, and laws to regulate railroad rates. Roosevelt obtains the Pure Food and Drug Act, the Reclamation Act and Employers' Liability Laws; above all, he strenuously concentrates his efforts on conservation, and the establishment of preserves for future generations.

1904 November 8, elected President over Alton B. Parker.

1905 March 4, Inauguration.

Roosevelt mediates peace between Russia and Japan, is awarded Nobel Peace Prize. T.R. quickly recognizes the new Republic of Panama, thus ensuring an American built Panama Canal.

1908 T.R. personally endorses William Howard Taft as his successor, securing his election.

1909 March 4, Theodore Roosevelt leaves the Presidency.
March 23, T.R. sails for Africa, to hunt.

1910 March 14, T.R. arrives in Khartum.
April - June, travels in Europe.

1912 February 25, Roosevelt announces his candidacy for the Republican nomination for the Presidency.
June, defeated for nomination by the convention, which again chooses Taft.
August 7, nominated for President by the Progressive Party (jocularly named the Bull Moose Party).
October 14, while campaigning, Theodore Roosevelt is shot and wounded.
November 5, defeated by Democratic nominee, Woodrow Wilson.

1913 Roosevelt travels in Brazilian wilderness, exploring the River of Doubt, which will later be named in his honor, the Roosevelt River.

1914 Archduke Ferdinand assassinated in Sarajevo, starting World War I.

1917 April 6, U.S. declares war on Germany.
President Wilson refuses Roosevelt's request to raise and equip a division of volunteers, for service in France.

1918 July, Theodore Roosevelt's son, Lt. Quentin Roosevelt, dies in France.

1919 January 6, Theodore Roosevelt, Jr., dies in his sleep in Sagamore Hill, at Oyster Bay, L.I.

* * * * *

Theodore Roosevelt, Jr., 26th President, had 6 children. By his first wife, Alice Hathaway Lee Roosevelt, one daughter, Alice Lee. By his second wife, Edith Kermit Carow Roosevelt, one daughter, Ethel, and four sons, Theodore, Kermit, Archie and Quentin. All four served in World War I. One son was killed, and two were wounded. The three surviving sons served in World War II. Two died while on active duty.

Compiled by Bryan Sterling

Theodore Roosevelt wrote over 50 books. The following are some of them:

Winning of the West, 1889–96
History of the Naval War of 1812, 1882
Hunting Trips of a Ranchman, 1885
Life of Thomas Hart Benton, 1887
Life of Gouveneur Morris, 1888
Ranch Life and Hunting Trail, 1888
History of New York, 1891
The Wilderness Hunter, 1893
American Ideals and Other Essays, 1897
The Rough Riders, 1899
Life of Oliver Cromwell, 1900
The Strenuous Life, 1900
Works (8 vols.), 1902
The Deer Family, 1902
Outdoor Pastimes of an American Hunter, 1905
Good Hunting, 1907
True Americanism, 1897
African and European Addresses, 1910
The New Nationalism, 1910
Realizable Ideals (the Earl lectures), 1912
Conservation of Womanhood and Childhood, 1912
History as Literature, and Other Essays, 1913
Theodore Roosevelt, an Autobiography, 1913
Life Histories of African Game Animals (2 vols.), 1914
Through the Brazilian Wilderness, 1914
America and the World War, 1915
A Booklover's Holidays in the Open, 1916
Fear God, and Take Your Own Part, 1916
Foes of Our Own Household, 1917
National Strength and International Duty, 1917